DATE DUE

MUSIC AND WOMEN

Frontispiece. A *Hekateion* unites the spirits of the
waxing, full, and waning moon: Artemis, Selene,
and Hekate. In this lovely ivory figurine from ancient Greece, dancing maidens invoke the three-fold
goddess to keep them in the flow of all life.

(See page 122.)

MUSIC
AND WOMEN

THE STORY OF WOMEN IN THEIR
RELATION TO MUSIC

BY
SOPHIE DRINKER

Preface by Elizabeth Wood
Afterword by Ruth A. Solie

The Feminist Press at The City University of New York

New York

Published 1995 by The Feminist Press at The City University
of New York, 311 East 94 Street, New York, New York 10128.

99 98 97 96 95 5 4 3 2 1

Library of Congress Cataloging-in-Publication Data

Drinker, Sophie, 1888–1968
    Music and women : the story of women in their relation to music / by Sophie
    Drinker ; preface by Elizabeth Wood ; afterword by Ruth A. Solie.
        p.   cm. — (Diane Peacock Jezic series on women and music)
    Originally published : New York : Coward-McCann, 1948. With new pref.
and afterword.
        Includes bibliographical references and index.
        ISBN 1–55861–116–9 (alk. paper).—ISBN 1–55861–120–7
        1. Women musicians.   I. Solie, Ruth A.   II. Title.   III. Series.
    ML82.D7   1995
    780'.82—dc20   95–14816
                                                                          CIP
                                                                           MN

The original text and pictures of *Music and Women* are photo-offset from the
1948 Coward-McCann edition.
Cover design by Dennis Ascienzo.

Material in the Afterword has previously appeared in the following publications,
from which it is reprinted here by permission: "Culture, Feminism, and the
Sacred: The Musical Activism of Sophie Drinker," in *Women Activists in
American Music*, ed. Ralph P. Locke and Cyrilla Barr, © 1995 by The Regents
of the University of California; "Sophie Drinker's History," in *Disciplining Music:
Musicology and Its Canons*, ed. Katherine Bergeron and Philip V. Bohlman,
© 1992 by University of Chicago Press; and "Women's History and Music
History: The Feminist Historiography of Sophie Drinker," in *Journal of Women's
History* 5 (1993): 8–31.

This publication is made possible, in part, by public funds from the New York
State Council on the Arts. The Feminist Press is also grateful to Joanne Markell
and Genevieve Vaughan for their generosity.

Printed in the United States on acid-free paper by McNaughton & Gunn, Inc.

CONTENTS

PREFACE

ALMOST fifty years ago, Sophie Drinker harvested the research of two decades in a pathbreaking book, a multicultural history of women's relations to music, sound, and rhythm. The radical concept, structure, and feminist insight she brought to *Music and Women*, which mystified or eluded critics at the time, has ensured for her work ever since both its continuing invisibility in professional music study and its underground survival—by word of mouth or hand-to-hand circulation of treasured copies—among women musicians and historians.

At last, The Feminist Press and the distinguished musicologist, Ruth A. Solie, with the support of Drinker's family, restore her feminist historiography, in its original illustrated and noted form, to general readers, music lovers, and women's studies classrooms. With the addition of Solie's Afterword to help focus discussion, *Music and Women* is used and valued as a textbook for interdisciplinary courses in women's history, cultural studies, and gender studies as well as for introductory music history and music appreciation courses, world music, and ethnomusicology. No teacher or student of "Women in Music" can begin without it!

Why do Drinker and her work still intrigue and lure new readers? How did this amateur musician at the age of sixty, a self-educated Philadelphian wife and mother, a well-bred "lady" of leisure and privilege, come to produce a progressive, activist work of scholarship? How is it that a work comparatively little known alongside other feminist texts of the time—by Mary Ritter Beard, Margaret Mead, Ruth Benedict, Virginia Woolf, and Simone de Beauvoir, for instance—should seem so fresh, inventive, and provocative?

As Solie brilliantly demonstrates, *Music and Women* seems oddly at home among recent histories of women's lives that go beyond individual, local, and national boundaries to incorporate varieties of cultural, political, social, religious, and sexual contexts in which women have both flourished and floundered. Issues and paradoxes Drinker posed in and for her work are as timely today as they were in the 1930s and 1940s for feminist theories on the place of music both in women's lives and the intellectual life of the West; the enforced silencing since Judeo-Christian biblical times of women in Western art music and its historical records; and the power and authority in and through music that women held and continue to hold in non-Western cultural settings.

Drinker's scholarship radicalized her thinking about the effects of patriarchal social and religious structures and ideologies on the cultural construction of gender and the writing of history. She had no interest in replicating conventional histories of "Great Men of Genius" for exceptional individual women and their musical production. What concerned her, first, were the varieties of musical sounds, dances, melodies, instruments, and collective practices women create in everyday life. Life itself, she believed, is sound and rhythmic motion. In her anthropological view of history, Drinker located powerful connections among female myths and rituals, the rhythmic cycles of nature and the reproductive and maternal female body, women's work, healing, and spirituality in homosocial communities, with a long tradition of female musicality, autonomy, harmony, and creativity in ancient invocations of the "feminine" in women's incantation, wailing, rejoicing, epic, and lament.

Second, in her sense of "divine discontent" with patriarchy and the intellectual and spiritual deprivation women experience under its controlling power, Drinker spurned conventional models of a linear, developmental history of music in Western civilization for an alternative, radically feminine prototype. Devoting more than half of her narrative to pre-Christian and non-Western cultures, Drinker conjured a cyclical narrative of female history modeled on the waxing, full, and waning movements of the moon-mother-musician-Goddess and her dancing attendants.

Drinker's musical philosophy, and her own musical practice, centered on the idea of a collective, participatory music-making in which ear and voice training and group singing could again become part of self-expression in the home, urban and suburban neighborhoods, rural communities, schools, colleges, public libraries, even playgrounds, as well as in professional musical contexts. "Where women are recognized as having authority to make music for important ends," Drinker believed, "where training, organization, and incentives adequate for the kind of music expected of them are provided . . . women living today are functioning as authoritative, creative musicians. No man makes their music for them; they make their own" (14).

In her Foreword, Drinker invokes the "daughters of the moon" (her original book title) to remind women everywhere of our "deep, and as yet in our world, untapped reservoirs of imaginative power" (xix). *Music and Women*'s lasting power may be in its evocation of what we have lost or are in danger of forgetting: a mother's voice singing a lullaby; the sounds of the gong, rattle, whistle, or drum heard and played in clamorous childhood; the rhythms and melodies our grandparents hummed; our ethnic and folk dances and songs; our multicultural musical heritage and sonic genealogies. Above all, her work invites us to experience again the joys and pleasures of music-making in our daily lives.

ELIZABETH WOOD

ILLUSTRATIONS

FOREWORD

MY ORIGINAL incentive to write a book about women in their relation to music came from a women's chorus that met for fifteen years in the music room of my home. It was my responsibility to find appropriate music for my friends who gathered here to sing—women like myself, neighbors with husband, children, and home.

From the beginning I was both surprised and shocked at the type of choral literature offered by the music publishers. It was childish, trivial, far too sentimental for these intelligent women who took time out of their busy lives for spiritual exaltation. It was, indeed, listed in many catalogues as music intended for "women's and *children's* voices"! I was amazed that the modern woman, with her high education, her personal liberty, and her active participation in the life of the community, was satisfied to sing, in a group, music manifestly inferior to other works of the same composers for solo voice or mixed chorus.

Almost none of the music we sang was composed by women. Why, I wondered, do my contemporaries, with their aspiration to self-expression, their notable attainments in this direction, neither excel as individual creators of the important music of our civilization nor even use a natural musical ability as a common mode of self-expression? Women musicians are experts in performing vocal and instrumental music, but rarely do they play or sing music that they themselves have composed. Why do they allow themselves to be merely carriers of the creative musical imagination of men? Why do they not use the language of music, as they use gesture and speech, to communicate their own ideas and feelings?

It is not necessary here to emphasize the value of music in relation to spiritual stature. Philosophers of all ages have dwelt upon the importance of music as both an outlet for the spirit and emotions and as discipline for the mind. It is generally recognized that music gives access to regions in the subconscious that can be reached in no other way. By plumbing depths where nature and spirit are in unity, a greater awareness of surrounding conditions may be developed and other inherent native talents may be stimulated into activity. Women's failure to think in terms of their own creative music has the inevitable result of causing a kind of feminine spiritual starvation. Moreover, it thins the quality of musical feeling and expression in general.

My intense interest in the enrichment of women's inner lives led me, therefore, from document to document, from book to book and article to article, from interview to interview with musicologists and specialists in other forms of learning related to this one, in my search for an understanding of women and music.

Among the countless things I wanted and needed to know were these, as illustrative: Had anyone undertaken a methodical analysis of early women's dirges and offered explanations for their composition? Did Victoria create his beautiful women's chorus "Duo Seraphim" for the Empress Maria and the nuns of Descalzas Reales in Madrid? Did ladies in medieval castles merely repeat songs improvised by men for their entertainment or did they evolve songs of their own? In modern times did American women play instruments with men in such musical groups as the Boston Flute Players Club? Where could I get the answers?

Grove's Dictionary of Music and Musicians was more of a puzzle than a source of information for my purposes. General histories of music rarely mention women. Wider histories of a general nature commonly ignore music while dealing with the "people." Fully half of the authors to whom I turned for knowledge, since they took account of women in connection with music, affirmed the passivity of women in this art except as inspirers of masculine musicians. Even in a book on *Woman in Music* carrying chapters headed Bach, Beethoven, Schubert, and Schumann, I discovered that women were depicted only as friends or relatives of these famous men musicians.

Yet I refused to be completely discouraged; I was firmly convinced that the whole story of music had not been told in a single volume, in any compendium of information on music, or in any collected series of works on the subject. I determined to find woman in this larger story of musical creativeness where I believed she belonged.

As I proceeded to read and to make independent inquiries, I did in fact find a great mass of material, both written and pictorial, concerning women and music. There were the rock paintings revealing women musicians. There were myths and legends about the musical activities of hundreds of goddesses and other feminine spirits—symbols and reflections of women in real life. There were the songs and dances of primitive women and of peasants. There were many references in scattered sources to Egyptian, Sumerian, Cretan, Greek, Roman, Chinese, East Indian, Arabian, and Jewish women musicians and also to the famous Saracen singing girls with their descendants at the court of the Great Mogul. There was proof of the participation of Christian women in the music of the early organized groups of Christ's followers. There were descriptions of women musicians from medieval times to the modern age. There were also musical scores demonstrating the character of a considerable amount of women's compositions.

From books in which this factual material appeared I have assembled, classified, and arranged pertinent items in manageable form. With my complete bibliography they may be studied in the Smith College and in the University of Pennsylvania libraries. The material on goddesses has been segregated for an article requested by the *Encyclopaedia Britannica* and will appear there in a forthcoming edition. It is my intention ultimately to make a reference book dealing exclusively with women's symbols and deities. Since pictures are indispensable in a comprehensive history of women and music, illustrations accompany each folio of collected material. Reinforcing the power of the written word, they positively portray musicians and they demonstrate the connection of women musicians with religious rites such as goddess worship and with the personal exuberance of women's spirit.

My distillation of facts for the present volume begins with four chapters on women as musicians in living groups of people called primitives and peasants. Why do I start with women of these types? There are two reasons: one is that the musical activities of such women, as in all modern researches for social origins, suggest the forms that prehistoric musical vitality assumed; the other is the clear evidence that such women are customarily on footings of equality or superiority with men in the realm of musical invention. In conformity with the practices of modern anthropological work, therefore, as well as with the findings that indicate a natural musicianship among women, the background of woman's musicianship in history is first brought to attention.

No doubt it is obvious that this volume is useful as an assortment of information about women's historic musical activities, but its true value would be missed if it were viewed merely in that way. Simply to cull items from it, as one might from a catalogue of musical events or descriptions, would be to tear apart things inseparably related; such as the intimacy between women's musicianship, their emotional reactions to productive labor, and their conceptions of the whole spiritual aspect of life, including their associations with men and children. Great music has always been rooted in religion—when religion is understood as an *attitude* toward superhuman power and the mysteries of the universe. This sensitivity to life, to its aims, its commands, its forms, and to its supporting emotions within men and women is a phase of the feminine being that, if deeply understood, should operate as an incitement to musicians, artists, poets, dancers, and all persons who long for a greater art expression in our modern world.

It is now nearly twenty years since I began to collect facts and to formulate ideas about women in their relation to music. During this long time, certain people have encouraged me beyond the point of polite interest in a neglected subject. Fundamentally, their support consisted in an understanding of my long and hard study in preparation for handling so difficult a matter, coupled with faith that the kind of book I had in mind could illuminate women's aptitude for musical composition, and induce in that light an impulse to more creativeness. From the beginning, the steadfast encouragement of my husband has been my greatest boon. His respect for me as an individual, creative in my own right, gave me the spiritual sustenance required for the expression of any original thinking.

For continuously challenging the validity of my interpretations and helping me to verify them from the authority of their own experience and knowledge, several women have my sincere gratitude. In that respect, Harriet Gratwick, Mabel Carnarius, Lela Vauclain, and my daughters live in these pages. In the early days when my project was in its infancy, Kathi Meyer, at that time librarian of the Paul Hirsch Library at Frankfurt am Main, opened the door to fruitful lines of research. Her wide musicological knowledge, so freely shared, has been a benefaction to me ever since. Katherine Swan, Russian sociologist and philologist, wrote for me an account of the participation of Russian women of all classes in music. Louise Beck, collaborator with Jean Beck in his work on the troubadours of France, gave me details about the musical activities of medieval ladies. Ruth Benedict, in the Department of Anthropology at Columbia University, taught me that woman's musical imagination depends upon the culture pattern of any given group for development as definitely as does any other human characteristic. The first to give me systematic editorial help was Katherine R. Drinker, at one time managing editor of the *Journal of Industrial Hygiene.* From first to last, Ann Chase has been constructively reviewing versions of the manuscript from the point of view of philosophy and psychology, and Catherine Drinker Bowen has as continuously given me the benefit of her great skill in the use of English. Mary R. Beard, who has written on women in long history but exclusive of the woman musician, warmly and generously reassured me that my efforts to introduce this feature of women's capability were socially important.

When I discovered that primitive women often displayed remarkable evidence of creative imagination, Heinrich A. Wieschhoff, curator of the African section of the University of Pennsylvania Museum, patiently answered a myriad of questions about rock paintings and primitive customs. More recently, M. F. Ashley-Montagu, associate professor of anatomy at Hahnemann Hospital in Philadelphia, checked my social anthropological data, and William Schuman, director of the Juilliard School of Music, approved the section on modern developments for the woman musician. The efficiency of Arthur Hamlin, assistant librarian in the service division of the University of Pennsylvania Library, in locating obscure books and articles has been a constant spur to continued research.

To Marjorie Barstow Greenbie I am indebted for final editorial services, which words cannot measure. Her long literary experience, coupled with Sydney Greenbie's wise advice, helped me to keep excessive details within bounds, to explain certain passages that might otherwise have been obscure to the general reader, to highlight several matters that I had perhaps underlighted, to add vivid touches from far-off places, and generally to give me confidence that my history of women in music would find popular appreciation.

I present my message, therefore, in the hope that it will remind every woman—and especially my own little granddaughters, Sophie, Ann, Ernesta, and Caroline—that they have deep, and as yet in our world, untapped reservoirs of imaginative power.

SOPHIE DRINKER

Merion, Pennsylvania
June, 1947

FULL MOON

CHAPTER I

SINGERS OF MAGIC

1.

WHEN the men of New Guinea are away at war, or on a long journey, their women beat upon booming gongs and sing to hasten the coming of the new moon. The first one to see the thin golden crescent in the sky gives a shout and all the women rejoice: "Now we see the moon, and so do our husbands, and now we know that they are well; if we do not sing, they would be sick or some other misfortune would befall them." [1]

No man composed the music. No man stands in the jungle shadows and waves his baton. No audience listens. But as the night silence deepens, and two or three tiny pinpricks of light in the village of thatched huts go out, and the young moon rides high in the sky, the voice of the leader soars as if it would lay hold of the very horns of the moon, and the voices of the others come in, rich and strong, supported by the rolling beat of the drums. The moonlight on their dark eyes and gleaming dark faces lights them into a deadly earnestness. They are not doing this to entertain anybody, even themselves. This is woman's music made by women only, for a woman's purpose. (See Plate 1.)

"If we do not sing our men will die." Theirs is an incantation or singing to invoke the powers that govern the rhythm of life. This moon that appears in the sky like a newborn baby will wax in the following nights like a growing child into a full round being. The women have power to invoke it with singing for the protection of their men, because they are the Daughters of the Moon.

Everywhere in the world simple, unlettered women who live more under the open sky than under roofs, without men's books, without men's churches and universities, feel their being as women peculiarly

3

linked to the celestial being of the moon. For the rhythmic drama of
a woman's bodily life, of which childbirth is the great climax, is
timed to the cycle of the moon. Her monthly cycle is four weeks or a
lunar month. She measures the time it will take her to bring her child
to birth by the waxing and waning of the moon. Ten times the thin,
gleaming crescent will appear in the sky, ten times it will grow to its
full, round, lusty prime, and ten times it will fade and shrink and so
grow old and die. Ten times it will be born again. And at the tenth
moon the child will be born, and grow like the moon to full splendor,
and wane, and die—to be reborn again like the moon, if a woman
has faith and makes the proper incantations or singing.

2.

Music in its elemental and primitive form, as still practiced by
people of the simpler societies all over the world, is incantation. Incantation from Latin *cantare*, to sing, and *in*, meaning into, is literally a singing into. The primitive musician believes that by directing
the force of rhythm and sound upon a thing, a person, or a situation,
he can make it conform to his will.

To any honest and simple mind looking out on the wild world of
living things, life is identical with rhythm and sound. A dead thing
does not make a sound. Its heart does not beat. Therefore life is
rhythm and sound. What is more reasonable than the application of
rhythm and sound to objects, forcing into them the kind of life one
wants them to have?

A Zuñi Indian woman making pottery, for instance, will imitate
with her voice the sound of water boiling. This is to make the pot
firm and unbreakable when water boils in it. Bavenda women pound-
ing grain imitate the sound made by their pestles—*gu, gu*—in the
mortars. Zuñi priestesses sing to the Spirit of Rain: "Fall upon the
mountains and on the plains!" [2] As they pronounce the command
they drop their voices in a descending scale to imitate the falling
rain. Lithuanian women imitate the sounds of words that are themselves suggestive of the rustling of winds, the gurgling of water, and
the trilling of birds.

In this primitive world there is rarely poetry without melody.
Poems are usually sung. When asked whether words or melody came
first into an artist's mind, a Hopi Indian said that song meant words
and music conceived simultaneously. Where texts of songs have been

written down by some visitor or literate scribe, an accompanying melody can therefore be assumed.

But this music has a practical aim. It is designed to do something. When a girl in Palestine thinking of her distant lover sings:

> "O trees, bend down to shade him,
> O stars, shine brightly for him!" [3]

she is making use of words to control the elements. And when a Greek nurse sings to a wakeful child:

> "The sun is sleeping in the mountains,
> the partridge in the woods—" [4]

her aim is to induce sleep by the power of suggestion inherent in the words. With us such words are merely poetic parlance. But these women believe them to be a practical method of attaining their ends.

As if to make their texts irresistible, women often end their formulas with words like these:

> My words, be strong and sticky, harder than stone,
> Stickier than glue or sulphur, saltier than salt,
> Sharper than a sword, stronger than steel.[5]

Out of the determination to make the words stick grows the musician's artistry. Rhythmical sounds and a variety of imitative tones reinforce the meaning of words and persuade or compel the listener to attend to them. So also do instruments. Women often make rattles by using gourds or by sewing little bags of dried skin and filling them with seeds or pebbles. They make pipes or flutes or stamping tubes by using hollow reeds or bamboo. They make the gourd zithers and probably the musical bow that in Rhodesia has nothing to do with the hunter's bow and is never used by men. Among European peasants women often use harp, dulcimer, and castanets; the tambourine is everywhere their special instrument. In many parts of the primitive world women not only use drums but make the drums themselves.

Except for drums, however, instruments are undeveloped in comparison to ours and exist generally for the purpose of making a noise to frighten away or to attract spirits. The voice is the instrument, and vocal music has attained in many primitive cultures a high state of artistic expression.

Just as it is obvious to the intelligent nature worshiper that life is rhythm and sound, and that if one directs the right rhythm and sound upon something, one puts life into it, so it is equally obvious that women are the proper persons to make incantations. Clearly women are more closely related to the life force than men, because they have the power to make new human beings in their own bodies.

Moreover, in some mysterious way this power in women to make people is related to the waxing and waning of the moon. Here, in the sky, waxing and waning, dying and coming to life again, is the magical prototype of life. And women, who make human beings, are obviously related to the moon in some special way.

So the woman's natural authority is the authority over life and death. By singing, she who understands human birth has the power to bring about birth everywhere. So woman's music is made in the stupendous faith that if it is only made in the right way, it can turn the old into new and bring the dead to life. There is thus concentrated in the single indivisible magic of a woman's incantation the foundation of the modern professions of religion, medicine, and music.

3.

I heard it while traveling—
The woman's song being sung.[6]

From the edge of the frozen tundra in the day-long night of the arctic winter, in Canada and Siberia, to the coral reefs of the Pacific and the green slopes of South Sea islands, which are like mountain peaks half sunk in the sea; from the vast hot spaces of Africa to old villages under the spruce and pine in Finland and Russia; from the foggy Aleutian Islands to Indian pueblos, under the blazing sky of New Mexico; in a thousand villages tucked quietly behind the peaks of the Andes, or forgotten on the slopes of Mount Olympus; in the valleys of the Himalayas and by the springs of the Yangtze and the Yellow rivers, or lost in the folds and crannies of Central Europe— brides, mothers, and old wives are making their own music. Blue-eyed or dark-eyed, pink-cheeked, olive-skinned, deeply brunette; Estonian women with smooth blonde sheets of hair; Indian women with dark braids; African women with tight curls, each oiled and carefully set; dark-skinned Melanesian women with bleached, bushy hair that is like a gold cap atop a vivid dark face—they are singing their incantations, their songs of joy and songs of sorrow. Through their compositions, in which words and music are of one inspiration, there resounds the story of birth, love, work, death, and rebirth, the story of hearth and home, the liturgy of woman's religion.

The primitive woman's authority over life and death, thus expressed in music, is supported by all the circumstances of primitive society.

Bringing life, fostering it with food and warmth, keeping humanity in touch with the spirit world are her normal activities. Her inborn talents all have a high value for the type of society in which she lives. What she does economically brings health and wealth to her people; what she does spiritually gives them contact with the life force. The more she asserts herself and the more she emphasizes her natural ways, the more power she brings to her tribe and the more she develops her own physical, mental, and spiritual stature. Childbearing, far from interfering, actually stimulates the development of creative imagination, especially her musical faculty. For around the physical nourishment and the spiritual aids that the mother must provide for the child, primitive family and social life are organized.

"In olden times, men and women were like two distinct peoples," [7] a Natchez Indian told an eighteenth-century French missionary. The primitive family is a considerable community of women and girls and boys under twelve, to which any number of men are more or less loosely attached. It is closely knit and self-sufficient, sustained by the women's monopoly of basic industry—the production of food and clothing. Women in primitive societies need no by-your-leave from their menfolk. They go about their business, not much caring what the men do, sure that when the time comes men will be drawn back to them by the irresistible double lure of sex and food.

Since primitive industries are centered in the communal household, the women must be well organized. There is the head of the group, usually the old mother or mother-in-law, who lectures the younger ones perpetually. She really doesn't know how she gets anything done with a lot of addlepated girls who are always planning to steal away and meet their lovers under the palm tree or the bamboo tree or the fir tree. She is annoyed with young women who are always mooning over their husbands or worrying about the babies. And she thinks the younger generation has no religion and never will learn to carry a tune or rotate their hips or shake their heels smoothly and rapidly in the community dance. Among the Maoris, where the grand old woman, work boss, priestess, and musician in one, functions at her best, she keeps after the girls from morning till night about their voices and the use of their bodies, while instructing them at intervals in all the other mysteries of life, and boring them to death with the recital of long genealogies. Thus, somehow or other, the new generation of women leaders and musicians is trained.

Subordinate to the old woman leader, but co-operating with her, are other older women, aunts, cousins, and females adopted into the household years before, down to the elder sister who is complete manager of the younger ones and responsible for all their sins.

Often women are organized into religious associations, or secret societies, by which they assert and emphasize their independence and solidarity. In certain African tribes today, women force men to remain in their huts during the performance of the secret rites. Men are convinced that their own vital powers would shrink up forever should they attempt to glance at the women's mysteries. In sex solidarity, women share their normal experiences, work in groups, play games together, help each other in childbirth, and worship their own spirits. Sometimes they speak in different language terms from those of the men. Wherever they dance, they use steps of their own invention, beat drums with their own rhythms, and sing songs of their own creation. (See Plate 2.)

Such institutions tend to develop women leaders whose authority often extends into the larger life of the community. As queen, chieftainess, priestess, prophetess, seeress, oracle, shamaness, magician, musician, and even as old wife who has experienced life, woman exercises a natural control over the members of her society. If and when women celebrate jointly with men at religious ceremonies and games, they perform as an independent unit with their own leaders.

Leadership in the fields where women have natural authority—in music, healing, and ritual—is strengthened by the attitude of the community. Among many simple people woman is highly valued for her natural bond with the life force. She is often regarded as the symbol of life itself. As long as the deep stream of mothers and daughters, bearing husbands and sons in its powerful current, flows on undisturbed, the spirit of the tribe prospers. Mothers symbolically pass the torch of life to their daughters; a girl in the bloom of youth with a moon tattooed on her back, a star on her forehead, and a turtle on her hands must dance to stimulate fertility in field and home. A May queen and a chosen youth must exchange the kiss that awakens life. Without the woman in action, there is no life *and the spirit lies dormant.* Woman's authority rests not only in birth but in the function of nourishing. Mothers are expected to feed their babies at the breast and then to provide other food. So women often identify themselves with the earth, or with grain, or with flowers and fruit. Some of the North American Indians call the corn "old woman who never dies" —the same name they have for the moon. Iroquois women regard the food spirits as their sisters and thank them with song:

> On the planted fields I walked:
> Throughout the fields I went:
> Fair fields of corn I saw there: . . . .
> I have thanked the sustainers of life.[8]

In one of the most beautiful liturgies in existence the Zuñi Indians glorify the nurturing mother. The Maiden-Mothers of the North, West, South, and East carry trays of seeds, each her own kind, as the wonderful truth is chanted:

"Lo, as a mother of her own being and blood gives life and sustenance to her offspring, so have these given unto ye—for ye are their children—the means of life and sustenance. . . . Behold! beautiful and perfect were the maidens, and as this their flesh, derived from them in beauty and by beautiful custom is perfect and beautiful, so shall it confer on those nourished of it, perfection of person and beauty. . . ."[9]

By reason of women's function as the source of food and drink for the newborn child, women are called upon to ensure, by charms and incantations, the water and the food for the community. They have authority over springs and wells, and often are the official rain charmers, passing on their magic powers to a daughter. Some peoples believe that woman's magic touch makes the grain grow. Among European peasants, where the formal ceremonies of the church have not completely superseded women's rites, women clap hands, shout, dance, shake tambourines, play pipes, and sing to celebrate the first day after midwinter and help call the spring and the season of new growth. (See Plate 3.) In Russia when spring is in the air and the birds are expected again, women bake buns in the shape of larks. Their daughters carry the buns out into the fields and call on Láda, goddess of fertility, love, and marriage.

> "Bless, Mother, oi! Mother Láda!
> Bless us to call the spring,
> To see off the winter." [10]

Many expect a priestess rather than a priest, or priestess and priest together, to serve in the religious ceremonies organized for the purpose of praying for prosperity. Great festivals are held at regular intervals and celebrated by men and women together for the purpose of inducing fertility, of renewing the warmth of the sun, of reviving the moon, of giving thanks for harvest, of casting out evil spirits, and of propitiating the nature deities. In some places, women and men beat the drums together and have dances in which both sexes perform. Among the Hootka Indians (U.S.A.) there are mixed choruses in which the men and the women sing in harmony. In other places women have their own dances and their own magic music. The women's choir, with its own leader, brings its own songs. For women to imitate men, or fail to make their own contribution, would be to defeat the purpose of their participation. This purpose is to assert and to emphasize the natural way of women in the scheme of life.

Women's authority over life and death extends to all matters affecting the security or continued life of the tribe. On this account some people even give women authority over the making of war. The Jabo tribe in Africa, for example, has two parliaments—the parliament of the young women and that of the older women. What these parliaments decide often becomes the law of the land. They decide that a stranger who wants to enter their country must not be admitted. And he is not admitted. They tell their men not to go to war and the men do not go.

To every people, war is both a religious undertaking and a practical task. Among primitive people it requires the services of women as the guardians of life. In their role of life givers they are indispensable to military victory. When the Haida Indian men go out to battle, the women sing and dance all night, pointing spears in the direction of the enemy. Women of the Karagive tribe accompany their men to war and beat the war drums. Scouting, fighting, inspiring men with courage, rejoicing at victory, lamenting the fallen, ensuring the continued life of their tribes, and performing different kinds of sympathetic magic with music are all activities regarded as normal for women in wartimes. (See Plate 4.)

Women's songs are valued as a means of transmitting strength to warriors. Among the Omaha Indians there is an old and untranslatable term, We'Ton waan, for those verses women sing in front of the empty tent of a man away at war:

"The timid leader never wins fame,
Let the tribes hear of you!" [11]

Through women the strength of the warrior may be preserved and transmitted to the tribe even in death. When an African Ibibio man is killed in battle, married women who are his next of kin rescue the corpse. No man may touch it. Weeping and singing sad songs, the scouts bear the dead warrior to a forest glade called owokafai—the place of those slain by sudden death. They lay him on a bed made of fresh leaves. Then they cut young branches from a sacred tree and wave the boughs over the genital organs of the warrior to extract his spirit of fertility into the leaves. Knowledge of the rites must be kept from men and from unmarried girls. Only married women, who have felt the virility of men in their bodies, can know the secret of life. To them it was entrusted by their great goddess "in the days when woman, not man, was the dominant sex . . . on the guarding of this secret depended the strength of the tribe. Were the rites once disclosed—few or no babes would be born, barns and herds would yield but scanty increase, while the arms of future generations of fighting men would lose their strength and hearts their courage." [12] This ceremony is conducted to the accompaniment of low, wailing chants, which only these wives of warriors have authority to sing, or even to know.

Even in places close to modern civilization the custom for choirs of women to sing the laments for warriors has persisted. On January 1, 1942, at Honolulu, when a funeral ceremony was held in memory of soldiers and sailors killed at Pearl Harbor, a choir of Polynesian women officiated. According to a newspaper account: "The silence was broken only by sobs and the soft chant for departed warriors sung by six native girls."

The association of women with war, and with music connected in various ways with war, is reflected in the fantastic figure of a terrible giantess. This Forest Demon of the Ibibios, whose women are so important in war and at the same time so musical, carries in her belly all the weapons in the world and also all the music. Bringing life to men engaged in a death struggle with the enemy and making appropriate music is thus impersonated by a woman spirit.

4.

The importance assigned to women in rites vital to the community stimulates women's musical talents. Because a woman is expected to give evidence of this life force flowing through her and because she has invented special powerful ways of using music for the benefit of her group, she is expected to make music. Primitive woman can be a successful musician because she is able both to realize and to idealize her natural capacities for work and for thought. Because her group demands music from her, she can assert and develop her native musical imagination.

Since women are expected to make important use of music, they have all the education in music the tribe can give them. Girls are trained in music and are given many opportunities for dancing, playing instruments, and singing. A girl lives her whole life among people who use music easily as a means of self-expression. She is as familiar with musical techniques as she is with speech and gestures. From the day she is born she hears the language of music and is taught to believe that it is a means of communication to be utilized at will. All children receive their first impressions of rhythm and melody from nurses, older sisters, mothers, and grandmothers. In many places, men initiates of religious cults learn the tribal songs and dances from the priestess in charge. Most primitive people regard women as peculiarly fitted by nature to think in terms of music; they consider music a direct extension of the functions of motherhood.

Talent and training in music are reinforced by adequate institutional support. Women's organization for making music is identical with their organization for the conduct of their worship, work, and play. The hierarchy of musicians consists of leaders, individual artists, and chorus. The chorus is the group of women who are performing their rites, working, or amusing themselves. The leaders and the professionals are the same women who have authority over the group in the ordinary course of daily life. The priestess-musician conducts the religious choir. The work leader conducts the singing of the women workers. In fact, a forewoman is often chosen for her ability to sing well and to have a large repertory of songs and stories. (See Plates 5 and 6.)

Both leaders and choir function under conditions that encourage them to do their best. Individual artists enjoy tremendous prestige and are often called in to perform at funerals, at weddings, and other occasions of community import. In North Russia, where the song leaders (*stihovóditzi*) are particularly musical, the chantress conducts the old rites and observes the old customs with authority often inherited through the mother's line. She knows by heart the ancient portions of the incantations and invocations that must be sung at every ceremony. She improvises new texts and new melodic lines to suit the emergency—a description of the virtues of the deceased, a history of the tribe, a portrayal of national characteristics, or whatever seems to be expected by her followers. The respect accorded her by both men and women is genuine, engendered by an inherited belief in her power to invoke the forces of life and by an admiration for her fertile imagination, which never fails to meet the artistic requirements of her group.

The women's choir functions at childbirth, at all rites of the rebirth, at work, at war, and for entertainment. According to local custom, the chorus sings in unison or in parts. In the Solomon Islands women sing thirds and fifths. In Papago Indian music a drone tone is held by women above the melody. Hottentot women often add a motif that, after an interval, they repeat with variations. An interesting type of part singing is performed by Russian singers. They develop variants to the melody, the effect being a rich harmonic structure quite different from the canonic imitation of western European polyphony. The responsorial form, in which the leader gives the first line of the verse and the chorus responds with additional lines, is universal. Antiphonal singing, which means that one group answers another group, is especially common among the Lithuanians, who, like many peasants, retain early customs. Among primitive women and many European peasant women the woman's chorus is as important a medium for the realization of women's musical ideas as is the solo singer. The solo singer's function is that of leader of the chorus. Though she may sing a portion of the song alone, she is primarily the spokeswoman for the group, who come in, rich and strong, with their own voices. The object of such singing is not the featuring of an individual, but collective expression under leadership.

Where women are recognized as having authority to make music for important ends, where training, organization, and incentives adequate for the kind of music expected of them are provided, primitive and peasant women living today are functioning as authoritative, creative musicians. No man makes their music for them; they make their own. No man leads them; they provide their own leaders. In their societies there is women's music—music conceived by women to fit their own experiences and to accompany their own activities. Women have their own dance steps, their own rhythmic patterns, and their own melodic lines. These are not, in any sense, imitative of men's, but spring wholly from the depths of their own approach to life and from associations lying deep in their inner lives. The explanation women themselves give of the nature of their songs is that some honored heroine or ancestress bequeathed the music to them, or else that they conceived it in a dream.

Though women imitate in their songs the natural sounds of the world around them, a man's voice is one natural sound that they do not imitate. In the entire range of the societies where women are creative musicians, instances of women assuming men's attitudes, taking over men's rites, singing in forced chest tones are rare and inconspicuous. On the other hand, instances of men wearing women's clothes, even castrating themselves, and singing in falsetto like women are, throughout history, frequent in men's religious ceremonies.

A complete collection of women's songs would fill many volumes, since, indeed, half of the folk songs and art songs of primitive and peasant people have been created by women, half of the total number of human beings. But our system of notation is, unfortunately, inadequate to reproduce them. On that account, many melodies to extant texts have been lost, or have become integrated into an ever changing musical idiom.

Wonderful songs and dances do not, of course, spring from every group of primitive people. Some races are not musically minded but develop their talents in other directions. Some merely make a noise with instruments and voice. But when a race is inclined to music, women as well as men, girls as well as boys evince the ability to think in terms of melody and rhythm, and even in harmony. It should be understood without laboring the point that women musicians of primitive and peasant societies are not to be compared to Bach, Beethoven, Brahms, and other musical giants of our civilization. These belong to an entirely different cultural level and cultural ideal. Primitive men are not creating harmony and counterpoint any more than are the women. But the music that women do create is of a quality and type entirely satisfactory to them and to their men, and is the highest that their culture knows. It requires for its composition, moreover, the same germ of emotional and artistic potency—the same capacity for symbolic thinking—that is required for the development of musical imagination at any time.

Most observers and historians of social activities in primitive tribes agree that the great school of primitive music owes its continuance to the woman musician. In both the quantity and the quality of music, women excel. Women dance more and sing more than men do. Women are the chief repositories for racial musical expression. It is they who store the incantations, the dirges, and the epics in their memories and who know the tribal lore. Women are also the chief transmitters of history, which is generally retailed in song and story. In the absence of written records, primitive music is passed on orally and often through the filter of woman's preconceived musical ideas, especially through lullabies and songs at initiation ceremonies.

Examples of primitive tribes in which women's musical activity is conspicuous in tribal life can be chosen from all types of humanity. Beginning in the north, the women of Kamchatka, of other aboriginal Siberian tribes, of the Eskimo peoples, especially those of Greenland, are outstanding musicians as compared to the men of their groups. In the Pacific islands, the Dyak women in Borneo excel in the music of their culture. The Trobriand Islanders, the Fiji Islanders, and many of the Maoris belong in this category. Among the black people of Africa the woman musician is in her element. Bushwomen, Pygmies, the Bavenda, the Ba-Ronga, the Valenge, Dahomeans, Ashantis, Wanyamwezi, the Tuareg, and many others represent woman's musical imagination in action.

Collectors of Oriental songs have commented on the extent of women's musical activity. In Tibet, for instance, and among the Dravidians of India, women musicians are outstanding. Grierson, who collected songs from different sets of people in India, said that he could not have performed his task successfully if he had not had access to the Hindu ladies' private quarters—the place where the old songs were remembered and sung. Women in Siam and Cambodia also excel as musicians. And Jewish women, wherever they live, have a native talent for musical expression. (See Plate 18.)

In the group of European peasants, women musicians stand out with undeniable power. Safarik, a prominent Slav scholar, said: "Wherever there is a Slavonic woman, there also is a song." A good half of the beautiful Russian, Yugoslavian, Bulgarian, Serbian, and Albanian folk songs are the product of women's imagination—their authorship in Russia being established by the use of verbs with feminine endings, such as *hodíla, trepála*. Fauriel, who collected Romaic folk songs, commented upon the fact that many of the most beautiful were women's songs. The folk literature of Greece, Finland, Brittany, Ireland, the Hebrides, and many other places is filled with women's musical poems. Latvian, Estonian, and Lithuanian songs are created almost entirely by women. In the vocal music of these countries men play an altogether secondary role. In Lithuania, especially, the bulk of the musical literature consists of the women's exquisite lyrics—the *daina*.

The manner of many European peasant women's singing is musicianship itself. The singers often have absolute pitch and are able to dispense entirely with instrumental accompaniment. Voices are true, strong, rich, and low. In one Lithuanian folk song a poetess-musician asserts herself with these proud words:

> What a sonorous voice I have!
> It is as if it flowed in gold.
> People from afar are listening.[13]

The group singing of both primitive and peasant women is completely satisfying to performers and listeners. Just as the women are sure of their own worth and confident that their music has a significance for the whole society, so do their rich, warm voices require no support from men or from instruments. The sounds produced by peasant women in chorus are extravagantly admired by both musically untrained listeners and musicologists.

Music created by these peasant musicians is marked by great vigor and richness of imagery, by highly ingenious rhythmic patterns, by a sensitivity to natural surroundings, by conspicuous beauty of melodic content, and by the same refined lyrical quality that graced the art of the ancient Greek poetess-musician.

The greatest heights of primitive and peasant music are reached in connection with those activities in which women have authority. No description, no recording, no evaluation of it can be made, therefore, without a recognition of the woman musician.

5.

It is easy for those who live within our own culture pattern to forget how large a portion of the human race is outside this way of life. It is also easy to take no notice of the fact that, as peoples outside the pattern of western European civilization that was dominant up to World War II bestir and assert themselves, they are not necessarily accepting the patterns that have prevailed in civilization up to this time.

All over the world there are still men and women who hold to the religion in which woman is the natural high priestess and maker of music. Many of these people are not to be regarded as uncivilized remnants of old races who will ultimately be swept into the currents of our present culture. On the contrary, most of them have been in touch with our civilization for centuries, and are now under the administration of some government that offers them all modern benefits —British, French, Dutch, Russian, or American. Most of them are nominally Christian, or are being actively proselytized by missionaries. They have educated leaders trained in the best universities of Europe or America. Withal, in really vital matters they keep to the nature religion and observe more or less the ancient festivals, of which birth is the central mystery and woman the high priestess, able by incantation or music to bend the unseen to her will.

One cannot see this nature religion anywhere in its entirety. One must put it together like the pieces of a picture puzzle—taking a birth rite from Africa, a puberty rite from central Asia—until the whole emerges. On the other hand, secret and unknown to most travelers as these customs are, incomplete, often quite archaic, one cannot underestimate their vitality. In the revolutionary ferment all over the world today, Christians with their roots in the woman's religion but with modern education are lustily reasserting themselves. This is true of the Maoris of New Zealand, whose Princess Te Puea is a genuine political force and earnestly calls for the maintenance of the rites. It is true in the resurgent Indian movement of Latin America, in Mexico and Peru, and it is true in many parts of Russia. In these movements, which are political and social and only incidentally artistic, there is usually a vigorous assertion of the values of that type of communal living in which women's talents as musicians and organizers of rites flowered.

It is true that the woman in these societies is not always a happy creature, that she often lacks freedoms her civilized sisters enjoy, and that she submits to customs discriminatory to her sex. Nevertheless, woman's authority as bearer of life is incorporated into religious dogma. Every individual woman in the tribe has an inestimable spiritual advantage. One of her great advantages is the assumption that the supreme life force may be feminine and manifested by women. She is not limited to one male divinity with no feminine religious officials.

In these lands where women make songs and folk tales set to music, whatever a woman does, what she is, and what she is valued for become projected into some kind of image or symbol. An outstanding woman becomes magnified and glorified into a goddess. When Queen Oya of the Yoruba died about two hundred years ago she was elevated to the rank of a divine power. Today homage is paid to her as the spirit of the giant river Niger.

Hardly a primitive or peasant society exists without its spirits who lead, protect, and represent women. For the Ibibios, the mother of the town is a huge tree. Generation after generation of little brown girls is presented to it. Often the guardian of women is a great rock or water spirit. Often it is the moon. Again it is a supernatural woman. Dzogbemesi—Woman of the Other World—receives the prayers of the African Matse mothers. She punishes all those who would harm her protégées, even their husbands. The Lithuanian Mahra, with loosened hair streaming on her shoulders, holds a woman in labor on her lap. Láda, in Russia, brings the flowers and fruits of summer. "Mother" and "love" are the same word in the language of the Ibibios. Over them there rules a great life giver, whose face is the face of love. This mother-love goddess—Eka Abassi—is such an overwhelming power that no man dares approach her or speak her name above a whisper.

Of all the symbols of womanhood, the moon is the most significant. The mysterious apparent synchronization of woman's monthly cycle and her term of pregnancy with the lunar cycle brings woman and the moon imaginatively together. There is a woman in all moon myths. Even in cultures where the moon is a god, the imagery includes woman either as the mother of the moon, as mate, or as daughter. Over and over again the moon is a god and goddess together—symbol of the growth and change that govern all forms of life on earth. But as goddess alone, the moon has many forms. She may be woman herself who grows and dies and is born again as a maiden, bringing with her the hope for the rebirth. She may be "the old woman who never dies." To the Polynesians she is Hina, the great goddess who has the power to grant immortality. To the Slavs she is Libussa-Baba, who invented birth and death, and who, as Golden Moon, eases birth. Or the moon may be a worker at any of woman's daily tasks and so unite in symbol the worker and the dreamer.

Behind the beauty and the romance of moon imagery flashes the vitalizing idea that woman is the special manifestation of the driving, untiring, *active* force of life. Of this the primitive woman's symbols and musical rites remind her daily. She perceives in everything that flows, that lives and moves and grows, something akin to her own power of growing and giving birth. The very word "rite" means a stream, a flowing, a manner, and a way. All through her life, in company with other women, she is asserting the special "way" of her sex and showing what good for the whole people can come from her work and her thoughts.

The men of primitive tribes know that woman's way in the scheme of life brings good. This conviction comes primarily from the practical results of women's working and thinking, which in simple societies relate directly to the fundamental needs of existence.

When the various rites of the mother's religion with its music and dance ceremonies are pieced together, a kind of composite woman emerges—strong, wise, creative by right of her womanhood. She cannot be seen anywhere in her perfection, though in fortunate and well-educated tribes like the Maoris there are women who very nearly approach the ideal stature of musician-chieftainess. But even when she seems to a Western tourist to be poor, backward, and greatly overburdened with work and babies, she may still have a kind of inner spiritual assurance that the educated and pampered woman of our civilization lacks. For hers is the inestimable privilege of *authority* in religion and song. And so the chief priestess of the Kwakuitl Indians sings, as she fancifully catches superpower from the air and throws it among her people:

> "I have the magical treasure,
> I have supernatural power,
> I can return to life!" [14]

CHAPTER II

BRINGERS OF LIFE

1.

*B*EHIND the music of women, in the simpler societies outside our present "civilized" culture pattern, there is a truly grand idea. It is an idea so obvious that it seems to have occurred to women everywhere, almost as soon as they were able to think in general terms and imaginative symbols. It is so fundamental and so universal that much of it has been incorporated into all the great religious systems.

This is the idea: that the process of birth offers the key to the understanding of everything else in life. As St. Paul wrote the Romans, "For we know that the whole creation groaneth and travaileth . . ." As Christ said, "Except a man be born again, he cannot see the kingdom of God." As Buddha said, "The life of an individual on this earth is but one link or cycle in an endless chain of births and rebirths."

One cannot understand the relation of women to music in our culture today until one understands in detail how the primitive woman centers music, with its ritual and healing, in what is to her the primary fact of human existence—childbirth.

The circumstances and associations of childbirth set the pattern of the music and inspire other rites of the life cycle, such as puberty rites and wedding ceremonies. By a process of symbolic thinking, simple, profound, almost inevitable, music that has definite associations with childbirth becomes the music for death. For except as a seed fall into the ground and die, as Christ said, it shall not live. And beyond this death, there may be birth if she who gives birth will sing in the face of death the song she made out of the struggle of birth.

Marina Núñez del Prado has expressed this idea of rebirth in a

21

powerful statue. (See Plate 7.) The Bolivian mother Aymara prays to the Spirit of Life for her dead baby:

"Give back the smile of my dead son in the waving wheat!
For his flesh, flowers in the strengthening grain of my fields!"

From this faith it is a short step to the belief that everything good and desirable may be thought of as birth into a new condition. So the song of birth becomes a magic for the fertilizing of the fields, for the protection of men at war, for well-being and success of all kinds.

2.

For the woman, childbirth is a profoundly religious and spirit-bearing experience.

Where there are no physicians and hospitals to take over, anesthetics to be administered, and trained nurses to preside with impersonal routine efficiency, a woman must depend on spiritual rather than mechanical aids. Nothing mechanical and scientific stands between her and the dark glory of the moment when in labor and pain, face to face with death, she battles for the new life. But all the unseen mysteries of the universe are involved. Evil ghosts hover to inflict pain. Good spirits may be invoked by incantations and ritual. And over all presides the great, brooding mother spirit. So, as a woman's time approaches, there are preparations as for a supreme religious rite.

Almost everywhere, women banish men during childbirth. They resent any interference and have been known to kill men who spied upon them. But in some cases they compel a husband to remain alone in a hut and cry out, as if in pain, while his wife, on her part, bears her baby in silence. Whatever the local custom is, a professional midwife, who is often the high priestess or shamaness or a magician, takes charge. The mother or other feminine relatives and the woman's neighbors and friends gather round. In societies where the girl leaves her own home and joins her husband's family, the mother-in-law and her relatives are called in.

Midwives and relatives busy themselves loosening hair, unlocking doors, and untying knots in the effort to remove any impediment against birth. They swing and dance to keep in the rhythm of life. Among the Fans of Africa, the business is so important that a special enchantress hides in the bushes near the place of confinement and chants an elaborate melody for hours. Even the pregnant woman sings. And, over and above the human song, goddesses imitate with divine melodies the "low-lying" mother's voice.

A Fox Indian woman says of the birth of her son:

> The child could not be born. The women who were attending me were frightened. They said, "We shall pray for help." My mother-in-law went to a woman skilled in birth. She boiled some medicine. She made me sit up and she spat upon my head. She gave me the medicine to drink. She began singing. She started to go out singing and went around the little wicki-up singing. When she danced by where I was, she knocked on the side. "Come out if you are a boy," she would say. And she would sing again. When she danced by she would again knock the side. "Come out if you are a girl," she would say again. After she sang four times in a circle she entered the wicki-up. "Now it will be born." Lo, sure enough, a little boy was born.[1]

In the Fiji Islands today women are famous as poetess-musicians and use their talents to help a woman in childbirth. At this sacred event they allow no man to be present. Escorting their friend to the bank of a river, they place her against a wooden support erected for the purpose. The chief midwife, who is also the high priestess of the tribe, kneels with palms upturned in magic gesture, as in Greece Eileithyia, the goddess of childbirth, is always depicted. She invokes the child about to be born. Around the two central figures the other women stand in a semicircle. They wave their arms to and fro in rhythm to her pains and sing with a sighing, wailing sound. The low notes are given first and then the sound swells up to a high tone. Another wail begins on the high note and drops down, to rise again in rhythm with the effort of birth until the child is born.[2]

Here is the model for that rite of symbolic birth which is to be found in so many religions. The wooden supports and the woman in labor suggest an altar on which is laid a token representing the rebirth—the bread and the wine, the flesh broken and the blood spilled. Here is not the derived symbol but the act itself—the agony of struggle for the perpetuation of life in the divine presence. For the mother looking up in her struggle to the soft tropical sky may feel that out of it an all-comprehending mother spirit supports her—an infinite mercy, who like the moon knows what it is to wax and wane, to go down into darkness and after three days to rise again. So nature, in this quiet place, makes of the birth chamber a church. The fronds of the coconut palms meet overhead like the intricately carved arches of a great cathedral. The still waters of the river amidst the jungle undergrowth are the baptismal font. The rich tropical odor of growing things—of ferns and flowers and ripe bananas and of the fertile earth itself—rises like incense. (See Plate 8.)

And because they believe that in themselves they have power to invoke life universal, these women have something of sacerdotal dignity. Clean-limbed and strong, authority in every line of her straight backbone and high-held head, dignified and formalized by the gold-tinted circle of hair, the high priestess is the intermediary between the real and the mystery. The attendants form the liturgical choir chanting the eternal affirmation of life.

3.

Unless deliberately stifled, as it is in the Fiji Islands, some audible expression of the muscular effort involved in child-bearing accompanies labor pains. In an Indian tribe of Northwestern America, the sounds made by women in childbirth are a kind of irregular crying or singing, half way between a whine and a melody. But whether a whine, a cry, a shriek, or a suggestion of a melody, the generic term for these sounds is "wail."

In the effort to insure propitious delivery, every power of invention is brought to bear upon the childbirth cry. For this is the cry of life, the woman speaking in her critical hour to the universal life. The proper management of the wail is thought to be so important that it is often strictly controlled by social and religious usage. The mother's sound may be re-enforced by the beating of drums, timed to strengthen the rhythmical contractions of birth. Sometimes the mother makes no sound but, instead, her friends or her husband cry out in her behalf. In Thrace and in some Celtic countries, the attendants, the husband, and all the family cry aloud when the child is born. In certain African tribes, women even pretend that a spirit mother is wailing when her child departs from the land of ghosts to become a human baby.

Everywhere in the world, women make their music by imitating all kinds of natural sounds—the songs of birds, the soughing of wind, the rippling of water. But the sound of the birth cry is the natural

1. Carl Lumholtz photographed native women for his book *Through Central Borneo.* The Dyaks believe that beating drums and singing attract good spirits. (See page 3.)

2. A photograph from Routledge's *With a Prehistoric People* shows Akikúyu women in a great assembly. According to the customs of this musically gifted people, solo singers improvise and the group responds. (See page 8.)

3. In a Russian painting, girls can be seen going from house to house, singing Christmas carols and *kolyádki*. (See page 9.)

4. A contemporary Pueblo woman of New Mexico depicts her companions performing the Wheel Dance, an ancient war ritual. (See page 11.)

Photograph by Melville J. Herskovits

5. Wearing silver ornaments like the horns of the moon, these singers of the Dahomey tribe of Africa represent the army of 10,000 women warriors, famous in former times. (See pages 13 and 40.)

Courtesy of Alfred J. Swan

6. Chorus of Russian mothers in the Esthonian village Gorodische sing their wedding ritual. The men listen but do not sing. (See page 13.)

7. Graven in stone by a Bolivian sculptress of today, Aymara is the symbolic mother raising her hands in the gesture that magically brings about birth. (See page 22.)

Courtesy of Marina Nuñez del Prado

Courtesy of Virginia McCall

8. Under the direction of an eyewitness, a Philadelphia artist has sketched a childbirth scene in the Fiji Islands. (See page 24.)

sound most distinctive of women, the most intimately associated with that supreme experience which is the climax of their physical life and the source of their religious thinking. The Fiji Island women —notable musicians as they are—bring to their incantations considerable technical skill and base their music accompanying childbirth upon a sighing, wailing sound.

In transforming the wail into melody, women have a great variety of methods. A musician may herself build a musical phrase around a recurring wail. Or she may make a recitative alternating with wailing by other women in unison. In Corsica, a chorus of women intone a chant. The leader leaps suddenly into the center of the group and wails: "Woe! Woe!" as was the custom in performing Greek tragedies. At death ceremonies, Iroquois women formerly divided into two choruses, one of which gave the long-drawn out sobbing wail while the other sang a melodious chant.

In this manner, women's dirges in primitive music were born. As an art form, they evolved from the cry of childbirth, and for musical existence, depend upon a sound natural only to women. Dirges and laments are noticeably absent from the repertoire of primitive men. It is the mother's business to bring life, even in death.

And for this purpose of bringing life women have also stylized the wail itself. One magician may give it a regular form with a crescendo to a climax, followed by a relapse into a slow, dragging drawl. A Nubian woman begins on a high note and drops her voice by thirds to a twelfth below the original note. Wailing may be considered an art distinct from singing and a wailer, often an official of high standing, may be praised for her appealing, or her grand, individual style.

The wail, in its stylized form, is used now by many primitive people and was used in ancient societies. It was developed by women for a particular purpose as an independent art but it is not music and never became music. From the simple wail, women also evolved the wail song. In company with melodies derived from other inspirations, this did become music and was employed with endless variation by countless women musicians for those many practical purposes for which primitive mothers need music.

4.

According to the imagery of women, all life is a series of births and rebirths that they are empowered to bring about. Sickness can be transformed into health; adoption can symbolically render a person a blood relative. Puberty, or mating, is birth into maturity; death is rebirth into another world; the annual growth of vegetation, or the new moon, is birth for other forms of life.

One kind of birth is similar to another, so that in some cases the imagery of the three great crises of a woman's life—birth, marriage, and death—become interchangeable. A dead Russian maiden is dressed in her wedding garments and her burial is attended by friends who come as if the ceremony were for the wedding. In a poem by a Greek mourner the bereaved parents implore their daughter to return to them but the girl answers:

"Nay, I may not, dear father mine and mother deep-beloved,
Yesterday was my marriage day, late yester e'en my wedding.
'Hades' I for my husband have, the tomb for my new mother." [3]

The human mother's womb changes into a tomb and death becomes a form of marriage. The idea of the poem was clearly inspired by womb imagery and derived originally from the reality of childbirth.

It is easy for us to misunderstand these primitive wail songs because, with our overintellectualized and overdepartmentalized approach to music and to life, we have lost the simple yet profound consciousness of the oneness of joy and pain, of birth and death, that is in them.

The wail alone, or in its elaborated form of lament and dirge, sounds mournful in our ears. To observers of primitive women who sing with tears streaming down their faces, as in the Maori *tangi*, it may seem an expression of inconsolable grief. But its intent is actually to ensure rebirth. The very word "dirge" comes from the Latin *dirigere*, which means "to direct." The dirge directs the vanished life on its way.

The peculiar mournfulness of this primitive wail music is due to two factors. Even for sophisticated audiences sadness is more artistically moving than joy. It touches deeper levels of the unconscious. It induces a more complete sense of release. The primitive woman early learned that an orgy of weeping brought relief—an idea later elaborated by Aristotle in his dictum that the function of tragedy is the purgation of pity and fear through representative pain and death. So the primitive woman artist makes the most of the wail song, prolonging it, building it up to climaxes of sorrow.

The other factor that makes the wail songs mournful is that life has in it much of pain, and pain translated by the woman musician becomes the wail. For the woman every change may be thought of as birth or rebirth. And every birth has its memory—or anticipation—of physical and emotional distress. Even at weddings, occasions for joy and hilarity, women sense the coming suffering inevitable to their altered state of life. Mating and childbearing, essential in bringing about fulfillment of life, have for women an aftermath of pain and sacrifice. Estonian bridesmaids sing:

"Make thyself fine, O lovely maiden—
and on thy head place the wreath of sorrow
and on thy brow the wreath of pain—
Quickly, quickly while still there is light
gird thyself—for the twilight is coming on." [4]

But, sorrowful as women's wail songs may seem to our ears, they have two characteristics that make them anything but depressing when rightly understood. One is the intent, already discussed, to induce rebirth and the faith that this can be done. The other is the periodicity, the rhythmic alteration of mood, which is of the essence of a woman's peculiar vitality. So women combine lamenting and rejoicing in one rite. It is a common practice in primitive tribes for mourners at funeral rites to wail for hours, even for days at a time, but to break every now and then into sudden bursts of rejoicing. They find the burden of grief intolerable, possibly, and release themselves in the cry of joy. Or they rejoice in anticipation of the rebirth and so hasten it. Some Russian groups today also have the same custom. At the festival of Radunitsa, the goddess Ustara (whose name became converted to Easter) is invoked. The people mourn over their dead, over the decay of life in general. Then they turn toward the east and rejoice.

Women's expression of the mood of rejoicing seems universally to involve the sound of the letter "l." It is often formalized into the phrase al-al-al, la-la, or lu-lu—familiar to us as the "alleluia" of Jewish and Christian worship. In the primitive and peasant world, women give the "l" refrain in their songs of joy. (See Plate 21.) Lully-lu is often incorporated into lullabies, which are incantations to persuade children to sleep and also little proofs of joy in them.

Friends of a Jewish bride in Palestine sing a song of good luck for the new husband:

> "May the eye of God protect you.
> Lu-lu-lu-lu-leschl" [5]

The high trilling tone they use, often pressing their hands on their throats to achieve it, suggests the origin of the word "ululate." But since "to ululate" actually means "to wail," it is the womb from which the cry of joy and the wail of sorrow both come.

In a remarkable example of the union of the cry of joy and the wail of sorrow, a Calabrian singer pictures death as crouching in a mountain defile and snatching a young girl.

> "Joy, I saw death! Joy, I saw her yesterday!
> I beheld her in a narrow way, like unto a great gray hound and I
>   was very curious.
> 'Death, whence comest thou?'
> 'I am come from Germany—I have killed princes, counts, and
>   cavaliers, and now I am come for a young maiden so that with
>   me she may go.'
> Weep, Mamma, weep for me, weep and never rest—no more shalt
>   thou await me." [6]

The idiom of the wail song, varied to suit the occasion but essentially the same in all primitive woman's music, is associated with a great variety of symbols and symbolic gestures. When the woman makes her rituals, she finds a thousand objects to reinforce with sympathetic magic the power of word and movement and tone. For almost everything about her tells of birth and rebirth. Everywhere she finds flowers—flowers that are buds, like little girls, and open and bloom like a girl into womanhood. They fade, but in fading set fruit, and out of the fruit comes the seed, which, when planted, grows and flowers again. In every way flowers are symbols, even to the many strange ways in which, in their shapes and their colors and their folds and secret places where the honey lies, they seem to be modeled after those organs which the primitive woman often looks on proudly as the seat of her power. So flowers are everywhere used in women's rituals. The Hawaiian girls, greeting the big ocean liner with song and singing it on its way out of port, wear great wreaths of fragrant flowers called leis, and hang wreaths about the strangers' necks as a symbol of loving greeting. In the Andaman Islands a young girl is given a flower name from the time of her first menstruation until her first pregnancy. And in Persian folklore, if a girl dies before her marriage she becomes metamorphosed into a flower.

Lights and water are, like flowers, full of meaning. Torches symbolize the light of the moon, which must never be allowed to die, for as the moon comes back, so life comes back. Mirrors imitate the still surface of a lake in which the moon can be reflected. Water flows from the mother's body. When the membranes rupture the child is born—hence the water of baptism and of other rites of rebirth. When the child is born, first comes the water, then the blood. Broken pots filled with red ocher symbolize the blood of the mother sacrificed at childbirth. Plumes and jewels are the child. That queer little figure which is the peculiar mark of the Maoris, with its eyes of gleaming blue-green *paua* shell, is the unborn child with the moonlight in its eyes. In shape, bells suggest the womb. Flutes blow the breath of life. Drums give the beat for the rhythm of the universe.

The movements of the dance often frankly glorify the seat of the woman's power—with that circling movement of the pelvis and rhythmic rotation of the hips which is the distinguishing technique of the woman's dance in the Pacific islands and southeastern Asia. Susceptible young men often find these dances seductive, and so, when danced by young girls, they are often meant to be. For it is the right of woman, young and ripe for motherhood, to attract her man. Yet the real concern of the girls is often only to perform the traditional movements well enough to escape the artistic criticism of the older women and often of the older men, who become connoisseurs in these women's ways. So many hours of tiresome practice have usually gone into the acquisition of this hip and belly movement that it often seems to the girl a chore the elders expect her to perform, with very little relation to her own personal desire, which is naturally to attract a lover.

So the Roratongan girl, clad only in a brief skirt of shredded bark, a brassière, and a flower, lifts her pelvis as high as she can and then keeps it circling to the accompaniment of her chant. It is as if her pelvis were an instrument on which she were playing. It is a kind of invisible music similar to the visible and complex patterns of movement with which the Maori girls often accompany their songs.

Whatever conscious seduction there may be in the girls' dancing, there is none in that of the real experts in the pelvis technique. When one of those middle-aged or really old women who greatly excel the girls in the skillful manipulation of pelvis or feet performs the dance of the pelvis, she has no notion of attracting any man's eye. It is to her the lusty assertion of the glory of her womanhood, the triumphant flourishing of the seat of her power. And when under the fantastic gold lacework of the Shewe Dagon pagoda, on those marble courts smooth as glass, the Burmese women dance with circling movements of hip and breast, while the torchlight flickers on their smooth, earnest faces and the scent of trampled flowers and fruit rises like incense around them, they are dancing not to please men or women or even the impassive gold Buddhas sitting in golden shrines, but rather to realize something greater—their own part in the rhythm of the universe.

Out of the importance of birth, which is the center of the woman's religion and the source of her power to invoke rebirth, grow the various rites of the woman's life cycle—puberty, marriage, family or tribal celebrations of birth, and, finally, death. Since a woman has such important functions to perform, she must be carefully trained and provided with spiritual aids in all the crises of her life. So the little girl learns her pelvic dances. It is even more important for her to have this seat of her power well exercised and well trained, flexible, powerful, rhythmically responsive, than it is for her brother to learn to flex his muscles, clench his fist, strike straight from the shoulder, brandish his weapons, or leap and jump in the war dance. The tribe might get along very well if men did not go to war. It could not get along at all if the women did not bear children. So the girl must learn to move her pelvis freely and powerfully and dance the pelvic dance as the sign of her fitness for womanhood.

5.

When a girl becomes physically capable of womanhood, she needs spiritual instruction, a ritual induction into her new responsibilities, a new attitude to herself. Running around, often playing with her little brothers, she is sexless, immature. These traits she must now shed as the snake sheds its skin or the butterfly its cocoon, and emerge a true woman, with a woman's personality.

Girls' puberty rites are held at new moon and the initiates dance all night and every night while the moon is waxing. Dancing, instrumental music, and special songs quite generally accompany the rites.

Just as for childbirth, women have their own hierarchy. The mother, the eldest sister, and other female relatives play their part. High women officials lend dignity to the ceremonies. The queen of the Ashantis, for example, has a silver stool modeled on the type of stool used by women in labor. Seated on this throne, she presides at the rites of the rebirth.

In some parts of Africa, puberty rites are controlled by the women's secret societies. The Bundu, in Sierra Leone, is one of the most powerful of these associations. Women called "Soko" know the secrets of life—of which music is one—and pass them on to the next generation. (See Plate 9.)

Certain musical instruments are associated with the girls' puberty rites. According to local custom, girls play drums, rattles, xylophones, horns, and musical bows. The Bavenda girls, who belong to a very musical race, have an orchestra made up of different instruments. They perform at the Phala-phala Dance, one of the initiates' rites.

Whenever women assume responsibility for the girls' initiation into womanhood, they have also the incentive to invent the rites, the dances, and the songs. They make the ceremonies a time for chanting long stories in which heroines abound, a time for singing incantations, invocations to deities, a time for lamenting the loss of their little daughters and rejoicing that a new woman has arrived in their midst. The time, the occasion, and the symbolism inspire creative musical imagination.

A typical ceremony of puberty, interpreted as rebirth into womanhood, is that of the Intonjane in Africa. This is usually in charge of the aunts on the father's side, who choose girls and women to help them. When the old moon fades, the initiate is led, with much ceremony, to a small thatched hut that symbolizes the womb, and there she is left alone during the dark of the moon. On the second day girls go out early from the village to cut soft grasses for the ceremony. The women and girls left in the village sing and dance from dawn till sunrise, celebrating the coming of a new woman, invoking all good upon her. On the morning of the third day they dance again.

After sunset on the night when the new moon will appear in the sky, women and girls cover the girl with a blanket, wrap her head in a veil, and surround her in a dense crowd so that no man may see her. They take her with singing and dancing and clapping of hands away to a distant hill. In the dusk, just as the slim, silver crescent of the young moon gleams over the African bush, they come back with her to the village, singing and rejoicing as if a new person were being welcomed to the kraal, and from that night to the night of the full moon she sings and rejoices with them. Both the older women and the girls are musicians. No man has made for them the music they sing to the moon. They have made it themselves, out of their own hearts, with their own skill, for their own woman's need.[7] (See Plate 10.)

Where girls have ritual preparation for womanhood under women's leadership and are adequately trained in music, their poetic-musical compositions are rich in imagery, full of allusions to the various devices employed to bring about the rebirth, especially flowers. The girls liken themselves to a bud, which only the warmth of love can open. Or they look longingly at a meadow and ask who will make them a wedding wreath. The songs are often made in the form of a duet between mother and daughter. The mother asks the girl what is troubling her and the daughter confesses her desire to rest in her lover's arms. Many laments voicing disappointment or loneliness and many love lyrics expressing devotion to the beloved belong to this group. Known as "maiden songs" among European peasants, they form an important and particularly beautiful group of folk music.

6.

Marriage, like puberty, calls for the women's talent in music making. A typical primitive wedding is one among the Pygmies of Africa. These slender little black folk—four feet high, weighing only about eighty pounds—are thought to be one of the oldest races on earth. Though they never arrived even at the agricultural stage of society, and live by hunting and fishing in the great, hot, tangled forests along the equator, explorers have testified that their intelligence is of a high order. They have a rich lore of ceremony and music; they are vivacious and witty, cleanly and fond of decency, order, and beauty in the details of their very simple lives.

When a girl is to be married, the clan of the fiancé comes to her village to take her away. The men set up enormous tom-toms. As the drums begin to beat, the bride retires into a hut with her mother-in-law and as many of her girl comrades as can crowd themselves in. The mother-in-law places in the bride's arms the latest-born baby of the village. The bride says nothing. Silently she gives the baby back

and turns away. At this all the bridesmaids begin to sing and the
bride bursts into tears. Her bridesmaids keep on singing the whole
night through. And while they sing, the bride must weep, even
though to keep the tears flowing after long hours she puts a pimento
seed in the corner of her eye. The songs of the bridesmaids are long,
and among them there are strains of great beauty, in which after the
manner of all ancient poetry the music is of one piece with the verse
form, conceived with it in a single impulse of the imagination.

Song of the Bridesmaids, African Pygmy Tribes

Counting your steps and turning no backward glance,
Reluctant your feet and with the slow tears falling,
Today with a troubled heart, with a heavy heart you are leaving,
The Bridegroom is waiting, maiden, reluctant, advance.

Here is the home you loved, your girlhood companions,
Here you played as a child, here you trod in the village dance,
You must leave it now, turning no backward glance,
With a heavy heart you must say farewell to your loved ones.

The Bridegroom is waiting, maiden, reluctant, advance.

Counting your slow steps, go, but keep with you ever,
Keep in your heart the treasure, the sandal flower
Plucked from your mother's garden, it will tell you:
"There they love me still and will love me forever."

Counting your steps and turning no backward glance,
Maiden, reluctant, maiden, reluctant, advance.[8]

There are tears throughout these wedding songs, like the soft
rhythmic sound of falling rain on the awakening earth in spring.

At a Russian bride's farewell party—her *devíshnik*—which she
gives for her bridesmaids the night before the marriage, the leader
starts to sing in a low voice and the others pick up her melody:

"Why are you here, my sisters? Why are you here, my white swans?
You have come, my sisters, for my last girl's party.

"My dear friends, maidens fair, the golden crown will be taken off
    my head, the red ribbons will fall out of my fair braids,
My freedom will cease to be."[9]

The bride herself, seated in the center surrounded by the bridesmaids, repeats the words of the song, but instead of singing she wails
—the stylized wail that is one of the earmarks of women's expression from time immemorial.

Bridesmaids' songs are both numerous and beautiful. There are
the flower songs, sung while the girls are picking flowers and greens
to decorate the house and to make the bridal wreaths. In the Cyclades they sing:

> "Adorn the crowns with pearls and flowers,
> The bride and bridegroom are the moon and stars." [10]

There are songs ridiculing or extolling the bridegroom; songs prais-
ing the bride's beauty, songs rejoicing over the bride's new estate;
and always songs lamenting the passing of girlhood.

> Happy she may be again,
> But never more a maiden. [11]

The older women and the professional song leader have their opportunity, too, for musical expression. Songs are sung while the food
for the wedding feast is being prepared, while the bride's bed is
made, while she is swinging and dancing her way into her new life,
while they are waiting for the bridegroom to come, while the house
is being decorated, while the bride is being washed and dressed. In
Syria, when the professional hairdresser has finished her work she
beats her little drums and sings:

> "O bride, be silent, your mother weeps,
> And your bridegroom and his friends rejoice!" [12]

Finally, the bride herself must sing, and in her song her joy is tem-
pered with unfeigned grief and longing. A Greek girl realizes that
her family will miss her as she will miss them—especially at the hour
of waking, at mealtime, and at family celebrations. She sings:

> "I leave my blessing on my home!
> Neighbors and friends, adieu!
> Three vials filled with bitterness,
> Mother, I leave to you!
> The first to drink at dawn of day,

The next in noontide heat,
The last and worst in festive scenes,
Where all but one will meet." [13]

Wedding music is women's music, made by the bride, her bridesmaids, her feminine relatives, professional attendants, and the special singers. In any age, in any culture, including our own, music to
accompany the marriage is a comparatively unimportant category of
men's compositions. All wedding songs by Greek and Roman men
were modeled on those of Sappho. Among primitives and peasants
today—especially in Russia—men rarely sing during the long-drawn-
out marriage ceremonies but are satisfied to listen for days to wom-
en's endless repertory. (See Plates 6 and 11.)

7.

When the woman feels the first sign of new life in her body, she
rejoices, again often with elaborate and interesting rituals. After the
child is born, women have a series of celebrations at which they
dance, play on instruments, and sing.

The desire of parents to present their offspring in some formal
manner to other men and women of their group and to whatever
deity they worship seems to be universal. In primitive societies the
mother, who has admittedly played the larger part in this new creation, participates actively. Sometimes the ceremony is a joint affair
between men and women. Often women exclude men and conduct
the rites alone, according to their own interpretation.

The Pygmies have both types of ceremony. When a son is born,
the fathers celebrate and sing their own songs of rejoicing. The
women join in the refrain with their cries of jubilation. The young
mother herself is, however, the most important person of the group.
Custom decrees that she perform the dance of life, not only for the
purpose of giving life to her own child but to bring symbolic regeneration to the whole tribe. To the accompaniment of the shouts of
exultation given by the other women, she dances into the center of
the open plot and imitates every movement of her recent experience.

For every child, son or daughter, the musically minded Pygmy
women have a special ceremony to present it to the moon, the symbol of the rhythm of life. Among the Pygmies, the moon is feminine
—Generatrix, She Who Creates. To unite the mothers with the moon

spirit, the women paint their bodies white and yellow and dance the dance of life. They sing their sacred songs to Mother Moon—songs that have never been heard by men, even by those of their own tribe. This is a secret ceremony, women's own business to make the life they have created secure on earth.

In the Baltic States—Estonia, Lithuania, and Latvia—antiphonal choruses of women welcome the newborn child. Among the Latvians, two groups of girl singers vie with each other and compete for the praise of the guests. Sometimes two girls sing sitting face to face and holding hands. The listeners accompany them. These choruses are renowned for their excellence and represent the most finished type of peasant art. (See Plate 12.)

One of the most common ceremonies for women after childbirth is the rite that reintroduces her to her normal life. As practiced in primitive tribes, it is associated primarily with the idea of a mother being a potent manifestation of the life force. At the time of childbirth the life force is believed to be present in such power that it might injure other people. Like a live electric wire, it is dangerous. Primitive people have a feeling that they must detach themselves from the supernatural after any event that seems to suggest supernatural agency. When, for instance, strangers insist upon photographing them, they hurry afterward to bathe in flowing water. Most primitive women have a special ceremony to detach a mother from her close contact with the life force. At such ceremonies they employ the customary rebirth techniques—drumming, dancing, and singing magic songs. Owing to the distortion of these particular rites in "civilized" societies, the original significance of the idea behind them should be understood by everyone interested in women's spiritual growth and in her opportunities to be a creative musician.

A mother in the state of confinement, and even a menstruating woman, is often called "unclean." This word is used in the sense that she has disturbed the ordinary course of events. Butchers are also "unclean," because they handle live blood; those who tend the dead are "unclean"; men and women who have just had sexual intercourse are "unclean." All of these people and their actions have had contact with the life force. But a woman giving birth has had the closest contact and has the most profoundly disturbed the normal course of events. It is a general custom, too, to allow a longer period of time to elapse between the birth of a girl baby and the ritual detachment of the mother from the life force than in the case of the birth of a boy.

This is probably because a girl baby must derive added strength from her mother in order to carry on with women's business. But in any case, the word "unclean" has not the significance of an unhygienic or dirty condition, nor does it have any connotation of evildoing. The rites of primitive women, invented by them and presided over by them, are definitely associated with the holiness of woman as the bringer of life.

8.

It is in the presence of death that a woman's singing is called to its highest functioning. To the primitive mind, death is rebirth into another world. Because women bring life, they are needed to assist the spirit along its destined path. Without their ministrations, a soul might be lost and remain suspended in mid-air without rest forever.

Mothers, sisters, wives, midwives, priestesses, and especially the professional singers are in demand as purveyors of life. In the Hebrides the midwife is called upon to close in the sleep of death the eyes she opened at birth, and to sing her incantations for the rebirth. According to locality, the professional mourner has different names. In Russia she is "the sobbing one" (*voplénitsa*); in Corsica, *praefica*, like the ancient Roman woman mourner; in Calabria and Sardinia, *reputatrica*, or the one who tells the story of the dead. The Irish women's leader takes charge and, calling her companions around her, begins the chant: "Cease now your wailing, women of the soft, wet eyes." [14] (See Plate 13.)

In many places men are excluded from death rites. In others, men participate but without the authority of women, who are generally called upon to beat the drum of life, to act out the mimicry of birth, to pour the libation, to swing, to dance, to wave flowers and green branches, to tell the history of the departed, to wail, and especially to create and sing the dirges.

Mourning ritual usually includes dancing and often swinging. Death is the principal one of those events in human experience that disturb the even flow of life. Affirmation of the will to live is therefore important. Swinging and dancing keep one in touch with the rhythm of the universe, and at the same time can be employed as devices to bring about the rebirth. Among the Dyaks of Borneo the professional wailer sits on a swing near the corpse and begs the spirits to guide the soul in the right direction.

The dance is capable of infinite variation and has been developed into many forms by the fertile imagination of primitive women. Among the Baronga, when a chief has been dead for three months the oldest woman of his family connection is called in as leader of the ceremonies. The men demolish the hut that was the former home of the chief and prepare a flat place for dancing. The old woman then dances the womb dance and imitates every movement of generation and childbirth in order to deliver his soul. Likewise, on the shores of the Gulf of Carpenteria (Australia) certain relatives of the dead person have the duty of performing the mourning dance around the body. Weeping and singing all night until they fall exhausted, the women stretch out their arms as if to lay the body in the earth and thud their feet upon the ground in rhythm. (See Plate 14.)

Of all the devices to bring about rebirth, the wail is the most important. In the Jabo tribe of eastern Liberia the wail is developed into a long and elaborate composition by the mourner, who is an official of very high rank, lawyer and historian of the tribe. She stands with the white sunlight and black shadows of this equatorial land playing on her polished black body. She is stately and tall, full of poise and dignity, for in her land women are persons of power. In the absence of written records, the vast store of tribal information is kept in the head of this woman official—historian, lawyer, and singer at funerals. Since she knows the background of all present events, what she asserts becomes the law of the land. No funeral of a man of property can be conducted without her.

At the funeral this personage presides while a chorus of women wails for hours. Then she takes the stage and, performing solo, builds around her own wail an elaborate composition. She chants the virtues of the deceased, describes the status of his family, enumerates its prerogatives, and reports on the extent of his property, modifying her wail and transforming it into a melody. She sings the names of the living men and women of the tribe; she sings the names of the ancestors, both men and women, from the beginning. She sprinkles the many proverbs in which the life wisdom of the tribe is concentrated at appropriate intervals throughout this musical discourse, and always she builds out of the wail her melody. To her, as to Fiji women in their childbirth rites and the Russian women at the *devishnik* or bridal ceremony, the primitive wail is an inspiration to musical composition.

In the effort to make the wail a living and developing art form,

satisfactory to their artistic instinct while performing its more practical purpose of invoking the rebirth, women are stimulated also to
poetic imagery. The best performers try to avoid stereotypes and to
make words and music specifically apply to the one who is mourned.
In Albania, when they mourn an unmarried girl they sing:

> "O joyless woman who hath never known joy,
> Who hath never fulfilled thine own life." [15]

When they mourn a mother they sing:

> "O spirit of the house within the very walls where you sat—
> There you left shining glory!" [16]

In Dahomey (Africa) the oldest member of the family has the
duty of watching the dead body with the widow. It is also her duty
to compose the burial song at the grave and another special song
when the grave is later revisited by the family.

An old woman weeps, amidst the leaves;
A white haired woman—O—weeps amidst the leaves of the forest,
And she says, the birds in the bush,
The life of these birds is to be envied.
How is it that man born into life has no more generations?
He has no more! [17]

Laments return again and again to the imagery of the rhythm of
life. An Arabian mother mourning for her son slain in battle sang of
days and nights endlessly alternating. A famous Polynesian poetess-
musician, when two hawks bore her tidings of her son's death, compared him to the moon:

> "Thou art a moon that ne'er will rise again,
> O son of mine, O son, O son of mine!" [18]

The poetic imagery includes the representation of divine feminine
beings who sing and wail. In the Hebrides a goddess called Grainne
personifies the "Love of Women." She it was who kept the death
watch over the hero Dearg and made the famous lay, still considered
a masterpiece of its kind:

> See, O God, how I am—
> A woman without heart forever,
> A woman without son, without husband,
> A woman without gladness or health.[19]

This is the model for the many songs of sea sorrow in the northern isles, always composed by women when their men are drowned at sea. Like dirges the world over, its air has the form of a wailing chant.

Beautiful and touching as these individual songs may be, the meaning of them is missed entirely if one thinks of them as lyrics of personal sorrow. The grand fact is not that the woman weeps, but that she has the privilege of a representative position at death for her family and her community. And she has this because, in herself, as the bearer of life, she is the symbol of life. This is a position to call out any woman's talents, to give spiritual power and cohesion to the women functioning in groups or choirs at a state funeral or memorial service.

In Dahomey, for example, an important occasion for music is the memorial ceremony held before the tomb of a former king. A woman's choir of fifty singers officiates. It was heard by Dr. and Mrs. Herskovits in 1935. (See Plate 5.)

From the point of view of musical style [writes Dr. Herskovits], the most striking songs [of the Dahomean culture] are undoubtedly those which glorify the names and deeds of the dead kings and living chiefs. Here is no impromptu performance, but rather singing of a quality that can only result from long periods of rehearsal . . . the leader conducts very like a choir master in our European civilization conducts his singers. Songs are sung in unison to the accompaniment of only a gong, and, to the European ear, the tessitura is almost incredible, particularly in view of the length of the skips which take the singers abruptly from the highest to the lowest tones of their range. The training of the chorus is also to be remarked, for judged by any standards of *a cappella* singing the technical proficiency of these groups of women in unison of attack and in dynamics of shading is of the highest.[20]

Such singers have technique. But they have something more—a deep spiritual composure. For there is something in death that brings out a woman's talent and peculiar quality of imagination. And to the communal celebration of death, to the great concourse of

Courtesy of Frances Jones Hall

9. While her husband made anthropological investigations, Frances Hall painted a Sherbro tribe initiation rite. (See page 31.)

Courtesy of G. Routledge and Sons, Ltd.

10. For his book *Sex, Custom, and Psychopathology*, Laubscher photographed Bavenda mothers inducting girls into womanhood. (See page 32.)

From G. Buschan, Illustrierte Volkerkunde

11. On an old cloth painting, Norwegian bridesmaids swing the bride into her new life. (See page 35.)

12. A seventeenth-century miniature shows professional women singers called "Domin" performing songs of congratulation to an Indian princess and her newborn son. (See page 36.)

Courtesy of the Boston Museum of Fine Arts

From Mrs. S. C. Hall, Ireland, *1841*

13. At a wake in nineteenth-century Ireland, the men listen while women perform the ritual wailing and singing that brings new life. (See page 37.)

Courtesy of the Australian National Research Council

14. In an article on certain Australian mourning rituals, Ursula McConnel describes how women dance, sing laments, and make gestures as if to bury the dead. (See page 38.)

15. In Borneo, mothers swing their babies to sleep. (See page 43.)

16. Stone figurines from archaic Greece represent women bakers, led by one playing the flute. (See pages 43 and 101.)

men and the gathering of official personages, they bring their natural authority. Having created and practiced their wail songs of rebirth in rites from which they exclude men, for their own spiritual support, they are in a strategic position to be called in, in power, under their own leaders. Theirs is the privilege of adapting their own music to the high occasion when their community as a whole wishes to make the woman's natural affirmation of life in the face of death. Other songs they may make for themselves; many of their dances and rites may never be known except to other women. But here they are called to perform a public duty for the spiritual reassurance of all. So the dirge, as elaborated by women out of the childbirth wail and out of their faith that all life is one, becomes women's most important and distinctive contribution to music.

CHAPTER III

WORKERS AND DREAMERS

1.

*T*HE great moments in the woman's life are not many. Rituals may be called for only once in a year or once in a lifetime. But a woman's work goes on all the time. If she did not work, her family could not live. In many primitive societies women work too hard. The hours are too long, the work often heavy and monotonous, performed against the discomfort of extreme heat, extreme cold, or, as in the rice swamps, in a perpetual state of dampness.

But whatever the work is, it goes more quickly and easily if a woman sings. Most primitive people sing at their work for the practical purpose of easing the burden, as all who have watched—and heard—the coolies unloading the cargoes of steam liners in Shanghai or Calcutta or Singapore know.

In the African community of M'Komis, women are known to be poor and inefficient workers if they do not sing. Among the Bantu, the organization of groups for communal work is definitely stimulated by the opportunity to sing in chorus. Tibetan women work harder and longer when they lighten their labor with songs. In Lithuania, where the lyric poetess-musican flourishes, a young man in search of a wife will spy upon the girls while they are working to find one who can sing especially well, so fixed is the idea among these people that a good singer is also a good worker.

Spirits and goddesses who reflect woman's power and woman's activity are often singers and workers. When Tibetan women draw water at the wells, especially during the ceremony of the Great Prayer, the Goddess of Government incarnates herself as one of them. In the guise of a working woman, Pal-den-Tha-mo teaches her companions the topical songs. Holda, a Teutonic goddess, was a spinner who sang loud and long as she sat at her spinning wheel. Those feminine spirits that appear in so many myths representing fate, destiny, and fortune are always spinning and singing. Men workers are apparently not deified as singers.

Women's work songs are legion. Though they frequently rise out of the patterns and rhythms of a woman's work—as in the case of spinning songs, for example—their real inspiration are the associations and symbols centered in the woman's deepest personal experience. All art is the unleashing of the unconscious. Save as the unconscious is released, there is no true inspiration. And the primitive woman deftly fits the words and musical tones that come spontaneously to her lips to the pattern of what her hands happen to be doing. In this process she has one great advantage over her civilized sisters. She works in her own time, in her own way, under the leadership of women. So no male philosophy stops the welling up of emotion from her woman's unconscious, and the same musical idiom that has been developed for the rituals of birth and rebirth serve for the work songs.

In some kinds of work, women sing alone. In others, they sing and dance together. Since most mothers rock their babies in solitude, lullabies are solo songs. The work of grinding corn at a hand mill is also customarily a solitary task. The songs sung at this occupation are solo and, as a rule, sad. But when women work in groups at tanning hides, making pottery, milking cows, making butter, harvesting grain, mowing, gathering nuts and berries, washing clothes, spinning, weaving, fetching wood and water, and many other tasks, their songs are gay and spirited. (See Plates 15 and 16.)

Often the workers enliven their task by a singing game. In some European districts, for instance, the spinners sit in a circle with the best singer, who is usually the most expert spinner, in the center. She improvises a verse and then throws her spindle to one of the girls, who must add another verse to the song started by the leader. Whatever the mood and the form of the songs, however, they are women's own production, flowing freely from a natural ability for self-expression in terms of music. (See Plate 17.)

It is a general custom for the work leader and the song leader to be the same person. Sometimes strangers are brought in with the idea that they will suggest new songs and, by imparting new life to the music, will also speed up the work. Mary McLeod, a famous seventeenth-century singer, used to row around in her own boat from one

little island of the Hebrides to another in order to assist the women
with their "waulking." In the islands today, women are still waulking,
as the task of tossing and circulating the cloth that comes woven
from the loom is called. Descriptions of the business show how
Gaelic women combine work and music.

At this waulking we were women only. . . . An old woman, one
of the two song-leaders, began to croon softly. And, as one listened,
a quaint refrain shaped itself, a theme fashioned in strong rhythmic
and melodic outlines, calculated, like a fugue subject, to impress
itself easily upon the memory. This was caught up and repeated
by the workers *tutti*. A verse phrase of more recitative-like character, perhaps consisting of only eight notes to eight syllables, was
then intoned by the leader, and this was followed by a second refrain, longer than the first, but again of a strongly rhythmical
character. This, in its turn, was caught up and repeated in chorus.
And now the leader sang the alternating verse portions only, leaving
the refrains to the other women. But the musical interest was not
yet exhausted, for the leader skilfully varied the verse themes, and
I have tried in vain to catch and note all the changes sung on a few
notes by one of these capable, practised folk-singers of the Isles.[1]

Women of the primitive and pagan cultures are remarkably rhythmical in their movements. It has been noticed that they walk more
steadily than men and that they move with measured motion while
engaged in work. In Madagascar, for instance, women working in the
field, making long furrows for planting rice, move all the time evenly
as if to a fixed beat. In the majority of primitive communities
women work under their own leaders apart from men, at tasks that
are their own by custom and tradition. The pace they set is their
own pace. The movements are convenient to them. The tempo
adopted by men in marching and rowing, for instance, would not
suit women, and the tempo of songs sung to accompany marching or
rowing would be different for men and for women, and therefore
quite individual for each sex. Every work song takes its form from
the rhythm of the work. The leader's signal is often incorporated
into the text of the song. Words like "ho" or "oi" or the repetition of
numbers—one, two, three, four—mean that the leader is setting the
pace for the work.

To make the work go well, it is wise to have a verse that is the
charm, or rune. Meaningless words like *ko-ko-ko-ko, ninna, ninna,*

or *lully-lu* constitute the magic added to the verbal and musical command. Women use these charms for everything that they do—for quieting children and sick people, for healing wounds, for bringing milk into the breasts, for tattooing, for building, for making and washing clothes, for tanning hides, for making baskets or pottery, for bringing their men home safely, and finally, most important of all, for charming the good and evil spirits believed to be perpetually hovering about.

The charms and incantations that a woman may employ are sometimes enumerated in stories of supernatural women who guard the incantations and bring them out on occasion. When the hero Siegfried woke Brynhild from her magic sleep, she gave him a reward in the form of a magic kit containing her incantations. "This enchanted box," she said, "is full of secret power; full of enchantment, of prayers, and of joyous words. With it, you can learn the runes to bring you victory, the runes of the philters which will ensure you the fidelity of the captive wife, runes to bring about pregnancy, runes for plants which will heal wounds and cure sickness. Such are the runes whose power will endure until the day which puts an end to the reign of the gods." [2]

2.

Many different types of song are created by women as they work. There are the lullabies; the satiric songs, in which women make fun of men; the lyrics, either love songs or nature songs; the laments; and the ballads and epics.

Lullabies and other songs to entertain children form one of the largest groups of women's songs. They are composed not only by mothers but also by nurses and elder sisters, who in many societies are charged with the care of babies while their mothers do more productive work. Songs to induce sleep invariably take an even, rocking rhythm and often associate the rocking with swinging on trees.

> Rock-a-bye, baby, on the treetop,
> When the wind blows, the cradle will rock.

Dyak mothers actually suspend their babies on the branches of trees, where they swing to and fro and listen to their mothers' voices blending with natural sounds of wind, water, and the trilling of birds. The subjects selected by women for the lullaby poems are usually directly related to the child or to themselves. Some mothers and nurses praise the baby and assure it of undying affection and protection. A Hottentot mother touches each part of her baby's body and commands it to grow strong and big. Many mothers compare the child to a flower or to a jewel or to the moon. Some sing of their own experience at childbirth:

"Peace, my child, be still and sleep, my love, my tiny one.
Pain I learned from you, learned such pain as only God and I can
    ever know, and she who stayed beside me and saw you born.
Peace, my child, and cease to weep. Peace, my child, be still." [3]

In describing Eskimo music in Greenland, Thalbitzer refers repeatedly to the drumming, dancing, and singing of the women. And when he gives an example of the musical aptitude of these interesting people, he uses a woman and the song she sings to her baby as an illustration.

Much more art is required in the rendering of a little children's song than one would think from looking at the notes or words. The whole of the singing is marked by the deepest feeling in the voice. The singer makes use of the finest modulations in appealing to the fantasy of the listening child. . . . A bewitching charm lies in the East Greenland's mother's lullaby tones which she hums as she rocks her child. She sways her body and croons a simple song of two notes, one very long and one short which is higher—the most primitive song in the world which may have remained unchanged from the earliest childhood of humanity. Generation after generation has been introduced with those tones which have formed themselves in the soul of the Eskimo woman out of the loneliness and wild monotony of the desert land.[4]

The Pygmies, too, have a rich spiritual and musical life with fully developed rituals for the life cycle. As we have seen, Pygmy customs provide incentives for both men and women to develop creative musical imagination. But nothing that the men produce in music has impressed the historians of these extraordinary people as favorably as the women's songs. The high point of musical achievement stands out in the lullabies created and sung by the sisters and mothers.

Satiric songs form another large group of women's musical expression. An illustration of good-natured raillery can be seen in a Serbian folk song that describes girls and boys at work gathering in the harvest. After the work is done the boys fall asleep exhausted, only to wake hours later and to find the girls knitting and singing, not tired at all! Songs sung when women and men work together are usually gay and cheerful, with sometimes a suggestion of sarcasm or playful derogation. The satiric songs of bridesmaids often insinuate that the bride is superior to the bridegroom or that the new husband will not dare to mistreat his wife on account of the loyalty of her family—a fact in many primitive tribes. In Dutch Guiana an established form of social criticism is maintained through poetic-musical compositions. Women publish their opinions of men by means of song. The fact that society gives a name—*lobi singi*—to the custom endows the women's music with importance.

Laments of various kinds are sung by women while they work. In the Cyclades the professional mourners practice their dirges and plan the improvised verses they expect to sing at the next funeral. Or a musician may express her own sorrow. An Osage Indian woman has a special lament she sings while weaving the rush mat that is to be used on the new shrine. Softly and flowingly she gives her cry of longing for her dead relatives:

> "You have left me to linger in hopeless longing—
> Ah; the pain, the pain!" [5]

In India, women have a set of laments that they sing while grinding corn. These belong to the group of incantations known as *raga* and *ragini*, which are believed to have a direct influence on the weather, the change of night and day, and even the shift of the seasons. In these laments, called *Bārah-Māsas*, the singer mourns the absence of someone she loves and devotes each verse to a month of the Hindu year, describing the particular kind of woe she feels at that season. In this way she lightens the labor of her work, and by causing symbolically the rebirth of the year, hastens the return of her beloved.

Work is a time for storytelling. The world over, women are famous for their ballads and epics, which they usually chant with interludes of song and instrumental music. Russians are particularly adept at this type of musical expression. On the huge Lake Onéga in the far north, women rowers are employed by the government for mail delivery. While making their rounds, which take many hours, they chant long sagas. Long ago other women like them were symbolized by Wotan's daughter Saga—divine storyteller.

The topics of these song-stories vary in accordance with varying folk customs or folk experiences. In a lovely Russian folk song a girl describes how she makes a flute:

> In the field, a birch tree stands,
>   *Lyóuli*, it stands,
> I will cut three sticks from the birch tree,
>   *Lyóuli*—
> I will make three pipes—
> The fourth one will be the balalaika.[6]

A Chinese tea picker sings the whole story of her life—how she is awakened by the sun, goes to work in the fields, looks forward to the evening, and so on. A large number of the ballads and epic poems sung by women refer to historical events such as battles, floods, famine, and to the deeds or love affairs of ancestral heroes and heroines. The whole of peasant life is portrayed in the Lithuanian lyrics (*daina*). Songs of the family cult have a name of their own in Russian—*semeíniya*. Songs relating to the ways of the people also have a name—*bitovíya*.

Another type of story is pure fantasy. Whenever an African Valenge woman starts to improvise, she says, *"Karingani was karingani,"* which means "Story of stories." The audience repeats these words over and over, as if to remind themselves that the tale is only make-believe. These are the legends in which mythical creatures appear. We call them myths or fairy stories. Flowers, trees, and animals talk. Heroes and heroines become identified with them or with supernatural beings and then perform incredible deeds. In the stories, the superhuman and the human women too are continually singing in the most beautiful way imaginable.

The Ibibios have a legend in which the naiad of a pool sacred to women came to the help of one of these skillful singers. There were certain days, so says the legend, when no one was allowed to go near the spring. But a mother was forced to break the taboo in order to get fresh water for a sick child. She was blocked on the way by the spirit of the trees. She made a song appealing to the tree to let her pass: "I pray you, open the road, and let me pass to the spring!"

When the spirit heard her lovely voice, he swept his branches aside. She hurried on but was stopped by a leopard. She charmed him, too, and induced him to move out of her way. At last she came to the spring, and she sang again more sweetly than ever, entreating the goddess to forgive her for breaking the rule. Moved by the magic singing, the naiad guarding the pool rose from the water and gave the mother permission to fill her pitcher.[7]

A favorite fantasy appearing in all parts of the world is the bird-woman, who may be either a wailer, a warrior, a dancer, or a singer. She is always endowed with magic power. It is common for mourners in myths to turn into birds. In Lithuania the verb "to cuckoo" signifies "to lament." In Africa the honey bird, or *schneter*, is said to be an old woman who, wailing, pursued her lost son until she was changed into a bird. Among the North American Indians there is a myth of a girl who, grief-stricken over her lost lover, became a songbird. In Russia the bird-women Sírin and Alkonóst rejoice and lament. Feathered creatures, half women, changing miraculously from one state to the other, have different names. In Russia they are called *vili*. They perform all kinds of superhuman feats and are akin to the Valkyrie, who, in Teutonic myth, bear the dead warriors to Valhalla. *Vili* steal the apples (symbols of fertility) from the magic trees that grow golden fruit. They have long golden braids; they dance, sing, and always love music. (See Plate 47.)

Other spirit women live in faraway lands where men can never go. On the mythical island of Tuma, near the Trobriands, there are hundreds of women ready to dance all night. In the Hebrides, the beautiful Binnevale, who was called the "Mouth of Music," lived in her own specter world where the sun never set, the wind never rose, and singing never ceased.

These mythical retreats for women have actual counterparts. Many primitive women have their private islands and mountain haunts to which they retire at times of menstruation, puberty rites, and childbearing. The fantasy is an idealization of primitive custom.

3.

After the work of the day is finished, people everywhere turn to recreation and entertainment. Especially on holy days and at festival times, men and women congregate in the public place. There they play games, dance, swing, tell stories, and sing. Village dances in the

Hebrides are often accompanied by an old woman singing the *port à beul*. This is a type of vocal music that the Gaels find more exhilarating to dancers than any instruments. Often as the merrymakers dance around a May pole or a bonfire, drums are beaten and gay songs are sung. But always music of some kind is indispensable.

Choral singing or instrumental playing by women frequently entertains men. (See Plate 18.) The Trobriand Islanders, who are devoted to music, have song festivals called *kamroru*. Women dress themselves gaily and sit on new mats spread out in the central plot of ground. Swaying rhythmically, they sing all evening while the men look on and listen admiringly. In Kamchatka, too, the women were once wonderful singers. A traveler, Stellers, who visited the peninsula during the eighteenth century, noticed that the women had unusually musical voices, that they made extraordinary modulations while singing, and that they sang in parts. He described how the women sat on the rocks, like sirens, and sang to attract traders coming from other tribes. Stellers was so much impressed with the women singers that he said their arias could be favorably compared to those of Orlando di Lasso. "As they sing, they become very calm and well-poised. From this can be seen their special genius for music." [8]

Swing festivals are another type of amusement enjoyed by girls and boys together, but with girls taking the lead. Wherever the swinging games are played, girls and women are the chief celebrants and the creators of the songs. In Lithuania, especially, where the poetess-musician is so conspicuous, the lyric poetry contains a large number of girls' swing songs.

Swinging is, with many people, a rite performed at times when a symbolic threshold is being crossed. The bride swings into her new life, men and women swing at funerals, when seed is being planted, when rain is needed. The Dyaks of Borneo use swinging in connection with both daily life and religious ceremonies. Mothers swing their babies on trees; professional wailers swing at a burial and sing the songs that will direct the soul to its heaven; old women swing at the planting season in order to secure the soul of the rice.

Even if the swing festival is dedicated to amusement, it is usually a seasonal affair, suggesting its ritual origin. In India the women swing during the rainy months. (See Plate 19.) In Korea swing songs are sung on the fifth day of the fifth moon of the year. In the Cyclades the swings are put up in Lent. In the region of the Seven

Mountains (Germany) flax harvesters swing at the end of October and the girls play a singing game:

> Where does the moon rise?
> Blue, blue, little flax flowers!
> It rises over that linden tree.
> Flowers in the valley,
> Maiden in the dwelling,
> O, gallant Rosa! [9]

This verse is repeated as many times as there are girls present, and the home of each one is indicated as the rising place of the moon, thus connecting the song with the moon rituals common to so many primitive and peasant societies.

Another set of swing songs incorporates the wail into the even, rocking rhythm. In Karpathos, Greece, a festival is celebrated on each of the four Sundays preceding Easter. Swings are suspended between the windows of the houses bordering the narrow streets and on them the women sit. The whole village watches, but only women and girls swing and sing the death wails for the crucified Christ.

Primitive women and girls also have their own amusements apart from men. Beginning at an early age, the little girls play singing games similar to our "ring around a rosy," or the pantomimic type like "Here we go round the mulberry bush." Those invented by the young Pygmies are quite remarkable. Some are imitations of the mothers' work, such as fishing. One especially fine exhibition of talent is a singing game imitative of a partridge calling her young.

Older women, too, play, dance, and sing for each other's amusement. They frequently have secret societies, or women's clubs, where they meet with their friends. Bushwomen entertain each other for hours dancing the *kokucurra*—flute dance—and playing their flutes. In Dutch Guiana the women celebrate with dancing and singing at birthday parties—*mati*. Formerly, specialists made stirring toasts of congratulation, using this incentive to develop their poetic-musical talent. In many societies women are famed as storytellers. Among the Valenge Africans the relating of both true and imaginary events is one of women's chief pastimes. The Baronga are particularly good at it and begin singing tales and legends when they are little girls tending the babies of the family. Names and photographs exist of more than one "distinguished historian." Primitive women often act out their stories like a play. The women of the Caroline

Islands have a mock war, when they paint themselves red, brandish spears, and dance, not as if in sympathetic magic to help their men to victory in battle, but as if in a drama.

In the peasant groups there is the same kind of play and entertainment. The Russians have their *besédi* and their *posidélki*—words meaning "conversations" and "sit-down parties." These are always gay affairs at which the girls spin, embroider their trousseaux, and play games. With infallible memories and boundless enthusiasm, thousands of songs are sung.

Games played by older girls generally involve courtship, love, marriage, and ideas relating to rebirth. In Russia they tell each other's fortune on Christmas Eve. They place a dish (*blyóudo*) on the table and put in it their rings, earrings, bread, salt, and three pieces of charcoal. The charcoal signifies the house spirit and sacred flame of the domestic hearth. Then they sing the dish songs (*podblyóudniya*) and take one object out of the dish with each refrain. If the ring is drawn out first, it means marriage. If the charcoal, it means death. Another game song (*igorniya*) describes the hiding of the gold. "I am hiding, hiding the gold," sings the leader as she places a gold ring, which symbolizes the sun hidden in the winter. A girl in the center has to find the ring and bring it to life again. From Easter until midsummer, Russian girls perform their rebirth rites. In one of these, Kastróubonka impersonates the sun. To imitate the natural decline in the sun's vitality during the winter, a girl falls down pretending to be dead. She is buried in a mock burial by the other girls and bewailed by them. They move around her in a circle lamenting. After a time, the dead girl comes to life and they all rejoice with special songs.

Where there are games and singing, there must also be a leader, and in the women's groups the leaders are women. One singer mentioned by a collector of Russian folk tales in 1934 was Doúnya, a young girl twelve years old. Her repertory consisted chiefly of fairy tales which she told to two little children of whom she took care. Doúnya inserted songs, spiritual verses, and dirges into her stories. Anna Antónovna was another song leader. This old blind singer had no home of her own but went around to the different houses in the village to help the housekeepers. She earned her board and lodging by spinning, but it was her singing that made her welcome in the morning while the work was going on and in the evening when the games began.

Here are the keepers of traditional lore, re-creators of the musical heritage of the past, composers of new rhythms and melodies in their own right—artist folk singers in the making. They might well serve as guide and inspiration for some of the new social and artistic stirrings of our own day. Theirs is a kind of music that women might well bring back, in a great fertilizing flow, into the music of tomorrow.

CHAPTER IV

VICTIMS OF TABOO

1.

*W*HAT has happened to the women of our civilization? Why are we not matching in creative output the simple women of cultures much less developed than our own? Everywhere in the world, outside the highly civilized centers of Western culture, there are women whose participation in music is active and creative. Women's contributions in the form of love songs, lullabies, dirges, ballads, and epics are among the musical treasures of an art that itself has recognition in the annals of human achievement.

Are we less women than these singers and musicians? We love, work, play, bear children, seek reassurance in a sense of oneness with the life force. We inherit a magnificent art of music. Why, then, do not women as composers make, on the level of our highly developed culture, symphonies, requiems, songs, dances equivalent to those that are created by women everywhere in other cultures? Why are we so inhibited?

Before we seek the answer to our own specific problem, we may look again at the primitive and peasant cultures. Even there we can see that women are not everywhere performing their own rites and making their own music. Tradition or custom determines what forms of ritual, dance, and music shall develop. Frequently, customs seem to be followed without reason. They are fixed by what is called "taboo"—a social habit that, once established, becomes absolutely binding. Taboo means that something or other "just isn't done."

Primitive people all have the same general approach to life, the same conception of what the right relation of men and women to the laws of the universe ought to be. Their customs, their ways of living, however, vary radically from group to group. Some, for instance, believe in monogamous marriage. Others permit a man to have several wives, or a woman to have several husbands. In some communities the birth of twins is regarded as a sign of good luck. In others it signifies some evil influence at work and the mother is forced by unwritten law to leave her husband and her other children and to go to a settlement where only women who have borne twins may live. Custom determines what kind of work is suitable for men and for women. In some societies women milk cows and make butter. In others only men tend the cattle. Sometimes women do all the fishing; sometimes they neither fish nor eat fish that is caught by men. Everywhere people abide by local custom, local taboo.

2.

In the large majority of societies both men and women make music and dance. Both have their ceremonial dances, songs, and instruments in connection with the work and the rites customary to any given group. It frequently happens that certain instruments are played only by men and certain others only by women—taboo being equally strong against either group. There are some tribes, however, where *only* women are the musicians. Because men are *not* of the female sex, they have an inferior status with the spirits, and are therefore not in the class preferred to make affective music.

Such a tribe is the Tuaran Dusun of British North Borneo. Among these people, women only are the priests. Upon them alone falls the task of performing the rites that, with music, are thought to be capable of propitiating evil spirits. Priestesses conduct ceremonies at the planting of rice, for producing rain, and for blessing the villages. Dividing themselves into two groups, the women dance back and forth as in an antiphonal chorus and sing songs in a secret language. In a neighboring tribe the women use a sacred rattle. It is hung in a bamboo receptacle at the door of each house. Only the women may handle it. The men are actually afraid to touch it. Men play a subordinate part in all religious ceremonies, their only function being to accompany the songs and dances of the women by beating the drums. Although these particular men are inherently as musically capable as men of other races, they do not break through the barriers imposed by custom.

The Wanyamwezi in Africa are people of a different race and cultural level from the Borneo tribes, and among them, too, men are at a distinct musical disadvantage. The word Wanyamwezi signifies "Land of the Moon," and this tribe is part of the great Bantu family in which women in general hold high position. Wanyamwezi women are very strong physically and from a distance can hardly be distinguished from men. They have the right to be elected chieftainesses. They have the right to be magicians and witch doctors; and as wives of chiefs, they have great influence on all public matters. Religion with the Wanyamwezi consists in worshiping the spirits of the dead mothers and fathers. It is the women's business to keep the living tribe in contact with these unseen powers. This makes them important and necessary in the spiritual life of the tribe, and out of their spiritual function grows their music.

Wanyamwezi women sing more songs than the men and institute more ceremonies at which music is required. They celebrate secretly at puberty rites with songs and dances. Men have no corresponding rites. Women make music for the marriage ceremony, music for funerals, and music for prayers in which mother and father spirits are invoked. They sing lullabies and have special songs to celebrate the birth of twins. As women do most of the work, they have many work songs, especially for the preparation of the beverage *pombe*. Choral dances for war, for traveling, and for the greeting of visitors are particularly beautiful. Moving their bodies back and forth, waving green branches, clapping their hands, these magicians charm the assembled company. Only predestined women are poet-musicians. Famous as composers of songs, some of them are very influential and richly paid by the chiefs. Women alone rank as official songsters and lead other women singers in chorus. Accordingly, they are encouraged from earliest childhood to cultivate their natural talent. There is obviously no reason why men should not have the same high musical status, but they do not. Men never attain the status of official poet-musician and do not compete successfully with the women. In every branch of music making, women excel.

In other tribes where men are in no competition with women, they frequently raise barriers between their musicians and a free expression in music. Among the Omaha Indians, for instance, men singers are trained to adhere rigidly to a rhythmic model for the chants of the Hon-he-wachi Festival. Since the Omahas are a very musical people, quite capable of inventing new melodies and rhythms, this restriction is clearly a taboo and has nothing whatever to do with innate ability.

From Ján Hála, rod 'Tatrami

17. A contemporary writer and artist has sketched girl spinners of the Slovak village Vežee at work. Boys, waiting to walk home with the girls, listen to the spinning songs. (See page 17.)

From C. Sachs, Die Musik Instrumente Indians und Indonesians

18. Nineteenth-century Cambodian women of the royal household play orchestral music to entertain the king and his guests. (See page 50.)

From M. A. Kheiri, Indische Miniaturen der Islanischen Zeit

19. Swinging is universally a rhythm to insure life. A miniature of the Kangra School depicts a seventeenth-century lady on a swing and her companions playing musical instruments. (See page 50.)

20. Arctic explorers see women musicians in action. A Koryak mother of northern Siberia beats her drum to protect her family from evil spirits. (See page 59.)

21. "Al-al" or "lu-lu" generally express rejoicing as in "alleluia." While hunters drag in a white whale, Koryak women dance on the beach and sing, "Ah, a guest has come, la, la, la, lo." (See pages 27 and 59.)

22, 23, 24. Rock paintings from the preliterate age depict women performing ceremonies similar to those in many primitive tribes today. (See pages 62 and 63.)

Courtesy of Methuen and Co., Ltd.

Courtesy of The Clarendon Press, Oxford

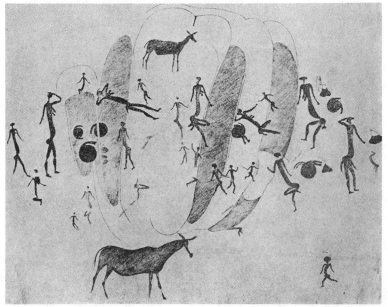

From L. Frobenius, Mdsimu Dsangara

Taboos of all kinds surround women and can often be traced to fear of their supposed contact with the supernatural. In some tribes women are officials, such as queen, chieftainess, priestess, shamaness, blian, doctor, rain maker, or magician, wielding real power, both temporal and spiritual. In others their responsibility is limited to the women's group and they are not called upon as public officials to translate their feminine power into benefits for the whole society. In still others women's organizations are comparatively weak. Women and girls have but little opportunity to work together in symbolizing their experiences.

Customs for women and music also vary greatly from group to group. It is frequently the custom for women to sing the songs in honor of ancestors. In other places they never sing them. Sometimes there is a taboo upon their playing the flute, or the particular type of drum used by men in secret ceremonies. In Surinam, for instance, women, the principal singers, never play drums. They believe that if they break the taboo their breasts will grow down to the ground. On Manam Island (New Guinea) girls are called upon to sound the single death beat but do not use drums at any other time.

The Caraja tribe of Bananal Island, Brazil, places a complete barrier between women and music. In this tribe it is the custom for women not to sing at all—not even lullabies for their babies. According to the cultural definition of singing, men only are the singers. When women wail and keen over the dead, the Caraja describe the sound—which we would call singing—by a word analogous to "croaking," a word used by them for the raucous calls of unmelodious birds. The Caraja word parallel to our word "sing" is used for the singing of men and of songbirds. Occasionally when women are working in the fields they attempt to imitate the men singers, but generally end by joking and granting that women cannot sing. Yet they have larynxes like other human beings and the same natural ways. Simply because they live in a society that does not expect them to be musicians and that deliberately discourages them from receiving training in music, they are forced by custom to pretend that music is outside women's sphere.

3.

Barriers arise from various causes. In some tribes, occupations around which music formerly developed have fallen into disuse and the accompanying songs are forgotten. "Meta, the Rikatha potteress, has given up the manufacture of pottery. All her pots cracked because, she said, she was the only woman practicing the art. In her former home, everybody made pots and the potteresses strengthened each other. When a pot was heard cracking in the furnace, somebody ran to the hut and collected a little of the dust on the floor and threw it on the other pots. It was too far for Meta to run to her old home." [1] And so no more pots are made. No more pottery songs are sung.

Or a taboo may be in force against introducing innovations in a traditional musical form. Such a restriction does exist among some of the African tribes where, although a woman has authority as a priestess over initiation ceremonies, she is under the prescription of a native law that deadens her imagination.

In other tribes particular types of song are never needed. Rowing songs, for instance, are not made by mountaineers. War songs are not necessary to peace lovers. Bridesmaids' songs are never sung where people make light of the marriage ceremony or omit it altogether.

Restrictions on sexual freedom before marriage naturally prevent a girl from composing wooing songs. When sexual freedom is allowed, however, girls may become the aggressors in courtship. In this role they create courting songs. In the Trobriand Island groups of girls with their faces tattooed make ceremonial expeditions to a neighboring village and, singing a ritual courting song, give signal to the boys of the village to approach. The two groups mingle and smoke and sing all night. Obviously, these courting girls, with no inhibiting tribal tradition of sex passivity, have incentives to compose love songs of their own.

Marriage is often a barrier that prevents women from either creating or performing music. The moonlight dances of the Akikúyu girls (east Africa) are never danced by married women, who express great surprise when the suggestion is made that one of them do so. A husband might say: "I have bought you and you want to go to dances!" Among the Annamites, girls are professional singers and dancers and are very much in demand at banquets or festivals, where they improvise for hours at a time. But opportunity for such performance disappears the day they marry.

A more formidable type of barrier between women and music in particular primitive tribes arises because women in those tribes are not in positions of authority and responsibility. It may be that men only are the chiefs, the priests, the shamans, the magicians, or the doctors. Men, therefore, have the incentive to invent appropriate songs and dances for the occasions where music is required. Among the Mescalero Indians, for example, priests rather than priestesses do all the singing at a girl's puberty rites. The same prohibitive factor operates in Bali, where the girls, although famous dancers, are taught and directed by men. Bali women are expected to perform, but not to create. Loss of leadership, or lack of a chance to lead, is a barrier to creative work that ranks second to none. The value of leadership to the composer cannot possibly be overestimated. It is the musical leader who has the opportunity to display artistic ability. It is the leader who can select significant poetic and musical phrases out of the many expressed by the less talented. It is through the leader that incoherent, incompleted utterances of immature artists are filtered and refined until they become art forms, acceptable to the whole group. Free and active participation in music making is, of course, a necessary condition to the possibility for leadership. But the mere singing, dancing, and playing of instruments in a group will not of themselves result in substantial creative achievement without the added opportunity of commanding the situation.

In the shamanistic cults authority may shift back and forth between the sexes. Shamans are individuals especially endowed with supernatural power to control the good and evil spirits. Shamanism is often identified with mothers, who, as chief guardians of family welfare and as chief interpreters of the supernatural, have the responsibility for controlling spirits who might harm or benefit their mates and offspring. Among the Koryaks of Siberia every woman has her own drum and her own individual drumbeat. Whenever any untoward event threatens to disturb her family affairs, she beats her drum and chants her magic formulas to frighten away the evil spirits. In this same tribe women are the official shamanesses, notable for their ability to keep in contact with the spirit world. Their primeval ancestress, Miti-Miti by name, brighter and more glorious than her husband, Big Raven, excelled him in cunning inventions and especially in the making of incantations. The real and the ideal women correspond. (See Plates 20 and 21.)

Among the Maidu Indians today, women are still the only shamans, and with their drums officiate as doctors and magicians. There are many other places, too, in which women are the shamans, notably in Kamchatka, where they are such fine musicians. Even in civilized Korea today a sorceress called Mu-Tang goes from house to house and by means of charms and music benefits the sick. Frequently both women and men know the art and are qualified to perform magic and to sell their musical formulas as we would sell medicine. In some places men have usurped the power of women, have taken over women's functions, and have become professional magicians. When shamanism becomes an affair affecting the welfare of groups larger than the family, men often exclude women from the professional group. They confess the higher qualifications of women for dealing with spirits, however, by dressing as women and by even imitating women's voices.

The North American Indians are an example of a large cultural group that regard music as the function of men rather than of women. There are many exceptions to this general rule, in the case both of individuals and of tribes. North American Indian women often dance, sing, and create music, but not to the extent that men do. When women are musicians, their music equals men's in quality and is often reproduced or mentioned by musicologists. There is no lack of musical ability, therefore, in North American Indian women, but a certain type of taboo prevents them from developing native talent. This taboo may be traced to the general custom of receiving dreams from the spirit world. These Indian men are expected to have contact with spirits, especially at the time of their initiation into manhood. When they fast and pray in solitude, they conceive music. These women, on the other hand, are not expected to receive messages from the supernatural. They are capable of it and frequently do, but just as frequently they are actively discouraged from such contacts. Among the Papago, girls who begin to show signs of mantic powers are forced to have their "shamans' crystals" removed. In this manner, a girl is directed away from developing creative musical imagination for no reason except that she is not a man.

How the different traditions for capability in music originated no one knows. Both men and women, however, made the customs in the first place or allowed certain prescribed manners to develop into tradition. Women, for instance, are not compelled by men to carry out puberty rites, which in many tribes involve some practices definitely damaging to the individuals concerned. Mothers and girls submit to being shut up in a cage for months after the first menstruation or after the birth of a baby. Nor is the separation of men and women in work and worship a state forced upon women by men. Women at times are aggressively antagonistic toward men and have been known to maul men unmercifully and even kill them for daring to intrude upon childbirth or other rites.

In connection with music, women sometimes themselves uphold customs that deter them from being musicians and probably often establish such customs. The Iroquois Indian women, for instance, who have a remarkably high status as mothers and tribal leaders, call upon men to be the singers at certain of the women's dances. Before the men begin to sing, they say: "We do this for our mothers." It has been suggested that long ago women needed the men's protection from enemies during the performance of the religious dances, and secured the men's services as watchmen by allowing them the privilege of singing.

Without the consent and approval of women, no cultural pattern could endure for generation after generation. Nevertheless, women often uphold cruel and senseless taboos that could be removed at will but which, while they are sanctioned, act as a bar to the free use of human energy.

The natural aptitude of men and women for musical expression is self-evident. But whether or not this natural aptitude is allowed to develop or to lie dormant depends upon local custom. As flowers flourish in bits of soil between rocks, so will musicians grow where even the least incentive exists; but where tribal custom dwarfs and obstructs, neither men nor women can create music, any more than flowers can grow under the shadow and weight of stones.

Has tribal custom dwarfed and obstructed the musical talent of the women of our society? Let us go back to the beginning of human records and allow the unfolding pages of western European civilization to tell the tale.

CHAPTER V

THE FIRST MUSICIANS

1.

*T*HE day that men and women danced the first dance, sang the first song, and beat the first drum will never be known. Who the first musicians were, where they lived, what motives and incentives led them to make rhythms and melodies, will forever remain a secret.

When the last of the great glaciers that had covered Europe for thousands of years was melting away, the warmth that came into the sunshine and the green that grew in the valleys made that age the real beginning of our history. The oldest monuments of human achievement that have survived are the paintings and carvings on rocks. Found in many parts of Europe and Africa in caves and on rock surfaces, protected by overhanging ledges, the finest ones date from about 10,000 B.C. Not all, however, are so ancient. Some, in Africa, are of quite recent origin. Yet the recent ones are so like the old that only an expert can tell the difference. A remarkable similarity in custom between very early peoples and those living in the same region today can be deduced from the illustrations and also from the testimony of the people themselves. The Bushmen of Africa, for example, interpret one rock painting as representing their Dance of the Blood—a charm against sickness. (See Plate 22.)

In some paintings women without men can be seen performing ceremonies of the sort that in present-day primitive tribes is accompanied by women's music. The women might be conducting a puberty rite or initiating a priestess. (See Plate 24.) One African rock picture seems to correspond accurately to a myth of the Australian Wikmunkan Ghost Clan, in which only the women know how to sing the mourning songs. According to legend, the ancestral husband and wife came to a tragic end and assumed the form of ghosts.

The wife sat weeping by a lagoon and made laments that her women attendants heard and passed down to generation upon generation of women.

The habitual secrecy with which our primitive contemporaries conduct their rites and the recognized authority of women in matters of birth and rebirth indicate strongly that designing and painting were also an evidence of women's magic powers and that many of the rock paintings were women's work. In certain North American Indian tribes of today, girls who are secluded during their puberty rites occupy their time painting pictures on the rocks. The midwives of Malacca, too, trace mystic designs—mainly flowers—on the bamboo tubes that hold the water they use for washing their patients. Only the erroneous notion of many nineteenth-century scholars that women do not function imaginatively has established the fiction that the pictures were all the work of men artists. (See Plates 22, 23, 25, and 26.)

2.

Everything that we can deduce by working backward from the present to these rock paintings suggests that the art of music may have begun in the singing of magic by women, and that women were the first musicians, and perhaps for some time the only ones. In general, the earliest forms of human society seem to have resembled those of the tribes that today have the least developed cultures. Some of the most primitive people today are very musical people— the Pygmies, the Bushmen, certain of the primitive Siberian tribes, some of the North American Indians, the Semangs in the Malay Peninsula, some of the Australians, the Tierra del Fuegans, and the now extinct Tasmanians. Semang men do not dance but are content to watch the women repeat their very primitive dance steps. Among the Seri Indians, only the women perform music. They have been heard singing simple melodies as they construct their rude huts of branches. They beat drums at puberty rites for girls and at death ceremonies. Bushwomen make drums and beat them. They play flutes and compose songs—especially lullabies and flower songs. The Kamchatkans and the Pygmies, as we have already seen, stand out conspicuously as creative musicians. Women of the Ona tribe (Tierra del Fuego), led by their own "kloket mother," perform a dance accompanied by a chant that is considered one of the rare examples of genuinely primitive music.

It is a striking fact that the women of the simplest cultures are more interested in religious ceremonies than are the men. In some tribes women only are the religious officials. In many, puberty rites for girls are conspicuous while corresponding rites for boys are lacking.

Again, observation of these primitive tribes today confirms the opinion now generally held by scholars that the earliest form of religion was moon worship, and the earliest religious ritual was a dancing and singing magic performed by women, with a view to influencing the potent power of the moon over life on earth. Today among the Pygmies the moon is feminine and is thought of as Generatrix, or initiator of life. The women of the Ona tribe (Tierra del Fuego) believe that Kra, the Moon Woman, came down to earth, lived with them, and taught them the ways of all women. This myth suggests that formal worship of the moon originated when women first observed that their own monthly cycle was synchronized to that of the moon and that the term of pregnancy could be counted by lunar months. There is, indeed, no explanation of the similarity of women's rites in all parts of the world except that they sprang from natural causes, common to all women.

Several myths represent a forcible determination on the part of men, at some point, to take over the women's magic moon rites. The Ona tribe has a myth that appears also in many other places. According to it, women had originally a pre-emptive right over the life of the spirit and over music. They once possessed the secrets of birth and death and spent their time discussing rituals and organizing choral dances. Often they dressed up like ghosts and deceived the men into thinking them supernatural beings. Finally, the men discovered the ruse and killed the women's leaders. Ever after, the men performed the women's ceremonies, excluding women from the stolen rites.

While this type of myth cannot be taken in the strictly historical sense, it reveals a state of envy—by no means limited to the primitive level—on the part of men for women's closer association to natural forces. Where men are known to have taken over mimetic rites that were originally the activities of women, as well as in many other cases where the history of the rite is not known, men often dress like women and imitate women's voices. This constitutes a clear recognition by men that they had adopted the magic devices, including the music that is inseparable from the rituals.

Just as religious music was probably made by women first, so the form of work songs probably originated with women. Such a development of musical imagination may be assumed from the fact that women are believed to have worked in groups long before men organized themselves for pursuits other than hunting and fighting—neither of which adapts itself to rhythmic action.

Whatever men may have done with music to suit their own needs in these earliest times, there is no question that all evidence points to the complete independence of women in music and ritual and to the general recognition of their special authority as life bearers in the making of singing magic.

3.

After the rock paintings, the next historical evidence of human activity is found in pottery vessels used for domestic purposes, mortuary urns, and little idols of men, women, and children. These have been excavated in the Indus Valley, in Sumer, in Egypt, and in Europe. They are frequently decorated with male and female symbols. The umbilical cord as the life line is a favorite design. Others are the triangle and spiral, which are also feminine symbols. Often vases were made in the form of a lyre—one of the oldest of the moon-woman symbols—or in the shape of a woman actually giving birth to a child. There are many figurines of women holding musical instruments—clappers, drum, cymbals, or flute. Other figurines represent women weeping or wailing. Most significantly, the images of musicians are generally female. Scholars suggest that the people of those times believed the images, when placed in a grave, to be capable of bringing about the rebirth by means of magic music.

These are often the earliest remains of truly civilized society, which began to be firmly established about 5000 b.c. in a few great river valleys.

Between 10,000 b.c. and 5000 b.c. the last ice melted in Europe. The shores of the Mediterranean were like a great garden. Where now there are only deserts in the Sahara and in parts of the Near East, there were meadows and flowing streams. And in Asia and Africa, as the earth settled into the warmth of our present time, great rivers built wide flat areas out of silt brought down from the mountainous centers of the continents. On these rich flats great numbers of people could live together and grow food for all. So in these river

basins the early primitive tribes, each clustered around its tribal
mothers, combined into large societies. These societies began to develop all those skills and comforts that are possible only where there
is a pooling of the power of many people for the needs of subsistence
and a specializing of skills. Instead of one primitive woman cooking
and weaving and raising food, people began to have cooks and bakers, weavers, herdsmen, and farmers.

Between 10,000 and 5000 b.c. such great communities were forming in four great river basins—in Egypt, where the Nile River brings
the black silt of the far-away mountains down to the sea, making
there the flat lands of the Nile delta; in the Near East, where the two
largest rivers of western Asia, the Euphrates and the Tigris, roll
down their topsoil and spread it in a great reedy, marshy swamp
and plain called Mesopotamia (or "Between the Rivers"); in China,
where the clayey yellow mud is brought down by the Yellow River
from the high peaks of central Asia and spread for hundreds of miles,
making soil of inexhaustible fertility; and in the Indus Valley, where
the earth from the Himalayas is rolled westward to the Arabian Sea.
Here the tribal families of the primitive mothers began to coalesce
and to build on a larger and larger scale, in more enduring materials.
The dried brick made of the river mud (what we call adobe) took
the place of reeds and wood; and then stone brought a long distance
down the rivers from the mountains took the place of adobe. By
5000 b.c. people were making things so enduring that one can find
today the remains of large cities and societies. In the same period
several forms of writing began to develop, and from that time we
know more and more about the past.

But what happened in those years when the primitive mothers
were uniting and linking their families to make cities and states?
Did they keep on singing to the moon and weaving songs of lamentation and of triumph? Did the primitive mother evolve with evolv-
ing society into the queen and priestess? And when there began to be
great religious ceremonies, with thousands of people participating in
vast temples with massive pillars of carved stone and hundreds of
lights at the altar, was there still a singing to the moon? And were
women as priestesses leading it? We have every evidence that this
was so, even in some cases down to Christian times, for in the first
picture writings, statues, and paintings there is the Moon-Mother-
Musician goddess in the full flower of her glory.

4.

This goddess, as she appears at the time when written and pictorial records become numerous, is the climax of a long development. She sums up and crystallizes what women did, what they wished to do, and what men believed they could do in the preliterate period when ancient mythology was being elaborated and handed down by word of mouth.

When about five thousand years ago unknown scribes began to write the first histories (in the form of stories designed to be sung), they told about superhuman beings who created the world, founded civilizations, and performed heroic deeds. In these epics women played a lively part, frequently a greater part than that attributed to men. To many people these deities of ancient times seem to be creations of poetic imagination with no relation to actual conditions. Gods and goddesses were ideal images, it is true, but the ideals expressed in them indicated existing values. A goddess standing on a crescent moon, for instance, represented the close association of women with new life. But at the same time the deities were generally reflections of the people—real men and women being prototypes of gods and goddesses.

The great driving energy that is the fount of all life was to many Hindus a female force. They gave it a name—*śakti*. In later times, in this section of Hinduism, every god had to be acompanied by his *śakti* and was often so depicted. Her energy manifested itself with particular power in the persons of the Great Mothers. They were sevenfold—the Seven Mothers, whose cult exists among many of the more primitive groups today. The large number of female figurines that come from the Indus Valley civilization suggests that a goddess-mother was worshiped three thousand years ago. In Egyptian history no time is known when four of the mighty mothers were not already there. Néït, the Weaver, thought to be of Libyan origin, had for title "The Old One Who Was When Nothing Was," or "The One Born before There Was Birth." Cat-headed Bastet had a name that meant Love. Nekhbiyet—Eileithyia to the Greeks—was the goddess of birth. She was the moon, the bringer of life. The Egyptians honored her by calling one of their towns after her. Hat-hor was "The Great One; eye of the sun-lady of heaven; mistress of all the gods." With the same authority, the Sumerian Innanna carried civilization and the arts to new centers. And under another name, the Great Mother in Sumer created the world and everything in it. The idea that woman gives the final touch which endows human beings with capability is also found in primitive tribes. It is an exciting one for a girl to realize and might well be incorporated into the teaching of history.

These goddess-mothers were generally represented as giving speech, music, and the art of gesture to humanity, and as being themselves dancers and musicians. The reason why the mother was thought of as the giver of speech and music may be easily understood if we again work backward from what we know of simple societies today. For where life is very simple, the baby is almost inseparable from the mother until after the age when it can speak and can begin to sing and imitate patterns of gesture. Mothers often carry their babies on their backs while working or while dancing and singing in religious ceremonies. The child drinks in speech and music with its mother's milk. So Bhāratī and Sarasvati, divine representatives of the dark-eyed women of early India, were thought of as giving all their people speech, music, and ritual. Sarasvati gave poetry and music and arranged musical tones into scales. Bhāratī taught the union of dancing with singing and is often called the Mother of the Bards.

In certain ancient invocations to deities, these two goddess-musicians were summoned with Ilā, goddess of the rite itself, and were spoken of as a group of three. Since they were deities of speech, gesture, music, and ritual, it seems clear that poetry, dance, and the occasion were enhanced by music and that they were integrated then, as they are now in India when the temple dancing girls add songs to their rhythmic gestures. The fact that these ancient deities were goddesses, not gods, implies that before their time women had been active in the making of rites, dances, and songs.

In Egypt, cat-headed Bastet held the sistrum and delighted in dancing and in music. Hat-hor, the Great One, was "mistress of the dancing, lady of music and wreathing of garlands, mistress of songs." They were matched by Innanna in Sumer, who was described as organizing rites, wailing to bring new life, lamenting over the dying year, and rejoicing over the rebirth. "She of the Beautiful Voice" made the lamentations and the incantations for the magic rituals. "O singer" are the words with which people began their appeals for mercy and compassion. The link between the real woman and the ideal in these representations was such a goddess as the Chinese Nukua. With her fine gold-tinted skin and tilted eyes, she has been identified as an empress, wife of the emperor Fohi. About 2500 B.C. these two interested themselves in making musical reforms, and to the Empress is attributed the creation of a tonal system for the use of musicians. In legend, the real woman became a goddess who mythically performed what the good Empress had already achieved.

5.

These oldest goddesses, spirits, symbols, and even names represent the type of woman normal for the period *before* written history begins. The women of the ancient world of seven and eight thousand years ago—in China, India, and on the Mediterranean shores—were themselves the prototypes of the deities. The hierarchy of divine and semidivine spirits represented the institutionalized role of women in that type of society. If a goddess was supreme in her circle, a queen and high priestess had previously had authority in her tribe or clan, settling a new territory, perhaps, selecting a sacred grove, finding times and places for the cult dances and songs. As the goddess Isis did, so might a queen have led the people to abandon cannibalism and to eat the bread she taught them to bake. If a goddess was able to help a woman in childbirth or to make grain grow by means of her incantations, then women had previously been skilled in medicine and in agricultural magic. If many goddesses danced and sang, lamented and rejoiced over the waxing and waning moon, or over decaying and sprouting vegetation, then many more priestesses had contributed to the development of those elaborate rituals and had been singing and dancing in choirs. There can be no doubt that women were creative musicians in that age which preceded the epoch of written history. Superhuman or human, women had economic and spiritual authority and could do what people expected to be done with music.

Women's religion, women's customs in primitive tribes, traditions handed down by men's secret societies, and the symbols of divine women in early mythology all point directly to the conclusion that men had not yet seriously put their minds upon the development of rituals, domestic work, and music until after women had established their own conception of a life of the spirit, including expression in music.

CHAPTER VI

QUEEN AND PRIESTESS

1.

*F*ROM about 5000 B.C. there are more and more indications of the way in which women were functioning as musicians. In the two greater river civilizations from which we draw our social and religious ideas—Egypt, whose culture was filtered to us through Greece, and Sumer (including Babylonia, Assyria, and Chaldea), whose heritage came to us through the Jews—the woman chieftainess and priestess-musician retained her high power for many centuries.

The spirit of the great civilizations of antiquity was the spirit of the primitive world, not of our modern world. Like simple people today, the ancients worshiped nature in its various manifestations as moon, as sun, as plants and animals, as the life-giving power of their great rivers. And like primitive people, also, they used music in a practical way to control their environment with sympathetic magic. Above all, they revered the special harmony of women with the rhythm of nature.

As civilization developed, religion, music, and the functions of women in connection with them were elaborated and refined. The forces of nature were personified by many goddesses and gods. Chief among them were the great goddesses, representative of woman's unity with the life force. When communal storehouses for surplus foods were built as a primitive form of social security, it was natural that the music and ritual for invoking the life force should center in these food houses. Gradually they developed into great temples, keeping down to Christian times some traces of their original structure and function as food houses.

Since woman's place in the scheme of life had purpose and dignity, public institutions were built around her natural functions, as well as around those of men. Women then represented in an official capacity the principle of female energy. Priestesses with their choirs of dancing, singing votaries functioned in the most important temples and in the most important rites, worshiping nature's rhythmic laws and striving to keep in touch with them by the techniques of primitive times, particularly by the dance and by music. But whereas in primitive times women appear to have carried on their rites separately from men, as civilization developed the tendency was for men and women to carry out their rites together. Many depictions of religious ceremonies represent a procession of men advancing from one side and of women from the opposite side, meeting before the altar in perfect equality.

2.

It is fortunate for our understanding of the early Mediterranean culture, in which our own civilization began, that its spirit and way of life have survived to this day in a mountainous region of the Sahara Desert. Here live the Tuareg tribes, thought to be the descendants of the once mighty Libyan nation, and believed to retain customs formerly prevalent in Egypt, in the Near East, and in Crete.

"She walks with her head high" [1]—a native proverb thus characterizes the strong-minded, gifted, and intelligent Tuareg woman, who is respected by the men of her nation in a manner that has no parallel in the Western world. These women have complete authority over the home and the rearing of children. They own property over which the husband has no rights. It is the custom for them to take an active part in public life, to be asked for advice in the tribal councils, to rule as chieftainesses, and even to lead the warriors into battle. Women are the preservers of tradition and learning. Where the ancient script, which has a similarity to the old Minoan script of Crete, is still used, women are more versed in it than men. Before marriage, girls enjoy great freedom. They are the wooers and often ride all night on their camels to visit their lovers. No household tasks are expected of them, but rather dancing, making poetry, and singing.

Music pervades the life of Tuareg women. When the explorers Denham and Clapperton visited the tribe over a hundred years ago, they reported: "In the evening, we heard numerous bands of females singing . . . this custom is very common among the people and is one of the principal amusements in the mountain recesses. They go

out when their work is finished in the evenings and remain till near
midnight singing and telling stories. The males seldom sing." [2]

At the present time it is the custom for noblewomen to organize
the meetings at which songs are performed and judged. The texts of
these songs are extremely varied, ranging from the love lyric to ballads of war and travel and to hymns of thanksgiving. Although men
and women both create the music, women are the more famous.
Some of them are known throughout the Sahara as the great creative
artists of this region. Women are at the center of these *ahaals* and
have evidently taken the lead in establishing them, just as the famous *salonières* of Europe attracted the brilliant men and women of
the eighteenth century to their own private houses. An *ahaal* often
takes place in the moonlight under a large tamarisk tree. The company gathers around the great fire. The women, clad in graceful veils
and heavy ornaments that might have come from the Bronze Age,
sit in a circle. Young men stand behind them and camels loom in the
shadows. A stringed instrument called *amzad* is played by the
women as they sing haunting melodies in a rhythm unknown and
indefinable to Europeans.

> "The heart thou lovest, and which loves thee not,
> Whatever thou do to strain towards him, he flieth.
> A sad torment for a thing it were better not to ponder.
> But if two hearts meet, it is heaven!
> It is better than all friends;
> It is better than the whole world!" [3]

The status of the woman musician and the attitude of men and
women toward the poetess suggests what musical customs were
actually in force in an age when goddess, queen, and high priestess
had a pride and spiritual independence comparable to that of the
present-day Tuareg poetess-musicians. (See Plate 34.)

3.

Protected by mountains and living off the main highways of aggression, the Tuareg probably represents a survival into modern
times of a fairly typical example of the light-brown race of northern
Africa that appears to have given our Western civilization its earliest
institutions. This race was widespread both in north Africa and in

From L. Frobenius, Mdsimu Dsangara

25. On the extreme left of this prehistoric rock painting, a woman holds her arms in the conventional pose of mourners. The Australian Wikmunkan Ghost Clan believe that the first lament was made by a wife for her drowned husband. (See pages 62 and 63.)

26. One hand of the prehistoric priestess rests on the seat of her power. The other holds a bison horn shaped like a crescent moon. A similar instrument is used today by the musical Valenge women to deflower girls. (See pages 62 and 63.)

Courtesy of The Hispanic Society of America

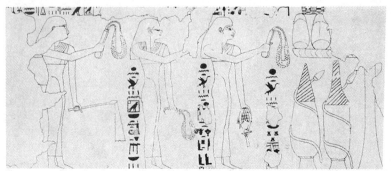

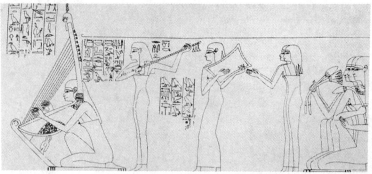

27, 28, 29. Egyptian wall paintings represented scenes of real life. Women musicians can be seen officiating at religious ceremonies. On the extreme right of Plate 28, the choirmistress holds her hand before her mouth, probably making the ululating trill. (See pages 76 and 78.)

30, 31. Cretan priestesses perform a religious dance before a great concourse of people, possibly invoking a feminine spirit to ensure the continuation of life. (See page 85.)

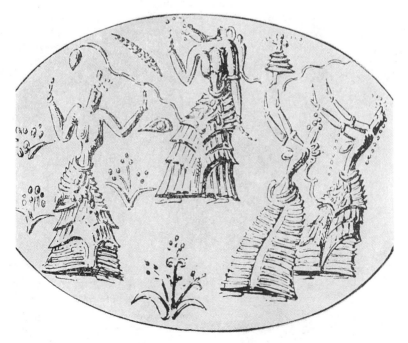

32. Cretan frescoes, like the Egyptian, reveal ancient customs. These choristers are boys, dressed like girls and led by a priestess. (See page 84.)

33. On a Greek vase, a chorus of women stands enveloped in a cape, the leader holding a tambourine. (See page 92.)

such Mediterranean islands as Crete. To it belonged the Egyptians, who have been called Hamites and are assumed to have been of the white race.

No civilization, not even that of China, has had a longer continuous existence than the Egyptian. From about 4000 B.C. to the conquest by the Moslems in the seventh century A.D. it had not only a continuity of life but a relative harmony and freedom from internal disturbance that indicated something very sound in its social organization. Egypt was distinguished for the high degree of comfort and beauty attained in household furnishings. All the arts of daily living were brought to a state approaching perfection. In some kinds of manufacture the Egyptians have never been surpassed, and rarely equaled. On the bodies in the Egyptian tombs there is linen of an exquisite sheerness. There was cloisonné of exquisite delicacy and perfection of finish. There were beautiful glazes on tiles and pottery of many colors—green and blue, purple, violet, red, yellow, and white. The manufacture of glass and the artistic use of it in inlays and mosaics was remarkable for skill, beauty, and originality. The same high standard may surely be assumed for music, especially since music was regarded by them as a direct and powerful magic for influencing spirits.

Egypt was also distinguished for the very high status of its women. As if reminiscent of a former matriarchy, royal power was transmitted through the female line. Every daughter of the Pharaohs was born a queen and possessed the prerogatives of royalty from the day of her birth. A man became king only by marrying a princess. In the later days of Egypt none of the sons of the royal house, however powerful, was allowed to forget that he held his right through his queen.

The custom of matrilineal inheritance made the queens legal and spiritual heads of the people. From the earliest times they undoubtedly had a large share in government and in affairs of the external world. As high priestesses, queens were identified with a local goddess, homage being paid to them in death as well as in life. Upon the death of the beloved Egyptian queen A'h-mose Nofret-iri (Eighteenth Dynasty), a special priesthood was organized to burn incense in her honor and to recite the formulas of prayers used in addressing the gods. When her mummy was excavated it was found to have dark-blue skin, the attribute of Hat-hor and Isis, goddesses of life and death. Immediately below the queen in rank were the other women whose husband was also the king. Custom allowed the king and other important men a number of lesser wives, who were princesses from neighboring countries. Some of the great kings had as many as three hundred concubines in their royal households. But these women were in a very different position from the concubines of later times or of some Oriental societies, for their relation to the queen as assistant priestesses gave them an institutionalized role in religious ceremonies and therefore a certain state dignity that can be acquired in no other way.

The position of ordinary women, who did not partake of the divinity of the women of the royal house, was, on a smaller scale, a replica of that of the priestess-queens. In the many legal documents that survive from ancient times in Egypt, this is emphasized again and again.

I acknowledge thy rights of wife [so runs one of those contracts]; from this day forward I shall never by any word oppose thy claims. I shall acknowledge thee before anyone as my wife, but I have no power to say to thee: "Thou art my wife." It is I who am the man who is thy husband. From the day that I become thy husband I cannot oppose thee, in whatsoever place thou mayest please to go. I cede thee . . . [here follows a list of possessions] that are in thy dwelling. I have no power to interfere in any transaction made by thee, from this day. Every document made in my favour by any person is now placed among thy deeds, and is also at the disposal of thy father or any relatives acting for thee. Thou shall hold me bound to honour any such deed. Should anyone hand over to me any moneys that are due to thee, I shall hand them over to thee without delay, without opposition, and in addition pay thee a further twenty measures of silver, one hundred shekels, and again twenty measures of silver.[4]

"Thou assumest full power over me to compel me to perform these things,"[5] declares a similar contract.

It was the custom for women to mingle in the general life of town and country, taking part in industry and agriculture as well as in trading. One of the boasts of Rameses III in the period of prosperity about 1200 B.C. was: "I let the woman of Egypt walk out to the place she wished, no vile persons molested her on her way."[6]

From the spiritual point of view, woman was generally regarded as being close to the invisible powers behind life and death. She could see and hear that which was beyond the perception of man. She could control the spirits with her flexible and piercing voice. Without a wife to influence the spirits, a man could not enter the gates of the future life. Many women, and not merely a few, therefore, played an active part in public festivals and in religious ceremonies. During the period of the New Kingdom (c. 1800 B.C.) scarcely one could be found who was not, or had not once been, a priestess or at least a minor official in the service of the deities.

The queen, as leader of women, was followed by an independent hierarchy of women—prophetess, spiritual teacher, priestess-musician, and choirs of dancing, singing attendants. The prophetess was regarded as divinely inspired; the priestess was the actual embodiment of the goddess she represented.

The priestess served both goddesses and gods. If priests served too in a goddess cult, they ranked lower than the women officials. It was the custom for priestesses to receive salaries from temple property and to be members of societies of scribes. They did not live in seclusion but attended to other normal duties. Many of them had titles such as "Worshiper," "Clothier," "Mother," "She Who Suckles." These names denote a high antiquity, an identity with the natural woman, and a precedent for the descriptive names frequently given to goddesses.

While the Egyptians were building their great civilization, making life stable, beautiful, and comfortable, they were never allowed to forget that the end of life is death and that beyond death is rebirth. Their genius and their wealth spent themselves lavishly on the tomb. Their religious feelings were expressed chiefly in rituals, incantations, and musical ceremonies intended to direct the soul on its way and to invoke the rebirth.

In conducting the rites for the rebirth, the indispensable priestess used the magic devices common to women the world over—holy water, the sacred ear of corn, incense, flowers; musical instruments, especially the sistrum; dancing, wailing, and singing. (See Plate 35.)

That the priestesses were trained musicians can be seen from their titles. A Fourth Dynasty name was Mrt, meaning priestess-musician. Another name given the woman conductor—Hnyt—signifies "Chief of the Female Musicians." Still another name was Phylarch, used in the time of the New Empire, when the priestess-musicians divided into *phylae*, or watches, for the purposes of attending to the music of the temple. From the time of the New Empire on for many centuries, chantresses increased in number and importance, being mentioned more often in the records. There were the "Great Players with the Hand"—always the hieroglyphic for singing; there was the "Great Chantress." Throughout Egyptian history she never failed to "content Amun with her voice." One of the most important, as well as one of the oldest, of the rebirth rites was the celebration of the Osiris mysteries. For this, priestess-musicians had special hymns of mourning for the death of Osiris in which his resurrection was anticipated. The priestesses impersonated the goddesses Isis and Nephthys— divine composers of all laments. They carried tambourines and sang both solo songs and duets.

Another important rebirth ceremony took place during the Sed Festival. This was celebrated for a dead king or other prominent man. According to an old custom practiced before the days of mummifying, a statue was made in the image of the deceased. While the statue was still in the workmen's shop, before it was dragged through the streets with crowds of wailing, mourning people, the priestess-musician was summoned to perform the rite of "the opening of the mouth" by means of her magic incantations.

A festival to ensure the continuation of life was the one named after Hat-hor. On the day chosen for its celebration, a choir of priestesses marched in procession, holding out emblems to bring health and wealth, blessing the people within their houses. In wall paintings these priestesses were depicted and designated especially as "the female musicians of Hat-hor, Lady of Dendera, Mistress of all the Gods." The inscriptions also convey the words they were supposed to be singing: "I offer to thee the *menat* necklace, the *sistra,* in order that they may give to thee a fair and long-lasting life." (See Plate 27.) Many religious ceremonies were conducted by priests and priestesses together. In the temple at Karnak bands of men and women musicians are depicted clapping hands and singing. Choirs of male and female musicians who daily sang hymns in the worship of Berenike are mentioned in a decree of Canopus. Celebrating the accession of Rameses IV is a line in a poem: "Maidens rejoice and repeat their songs of gladness. . . ." [7]

Throughout Egyptian history there is evidence in written documents, in pictures, and in statuary of women participating to the fullest extent in the religious ceremony and in the music accompanying it. As goddess, as priestess, as magician, as wailer, as choir leader, as choral singer, as dancer, and as instrumental player, women were there in the temples on an equality with men and often in a superior position to men. Often, indeed, the great temples, with their thick walls and massive columns, reproduced in stone the pattern of those huts made of reeds tied together that African women everywhere still construct with their own hands for their homes. And the elaborate ceremonies conducted in them retained a homely memory of the household life of women. More than one scholar has quoted the hymn:

> Awake in peace, thou cleansed one, in peace!
>
> . . .
>
> Thou sleepest in the barque of evening,
> Thou awakest in the barque in the morning [8]

as an example of similarity in practice in ordinary living and in temple service. These are supposed to be the words sung by the women of primitive Egypt for the purpose of rousing their chief in the morning. In later centuries, when the king impersonated the sun god in the temple, the same hymn was used by the priestess-musicians in the "House of the Morning" as a ritual for the ceremonial morning rebirth.

A similar association between the temple service and home practice can be seen in childbirth rites. In the pyramid temple of Sahuri —where the pyramid form itself resembles the female symbol of the triangle—priestesses impersonated Nekhbiyet, goddess of childbirth like the Greek Eileithyia, with whom magic formulas and incantations for aid in childbirth were immemorially identified. Egyptian women must have made such incantations, just as primitive women do today, or royal births would not have been described in legends in which Isis, the cunning magician, and three other deities appeared disguised as musicians to assist the queen in her need.

Songs sung by women in connection with other home events have been preserved and show the same belief that characterizes all primitive music in the magic properties of an incantation:

> Keep away from his teeth—they will bite you!
> Keep away from his navel—it is the morning star! [9]

Every part of the little body is mentioned in this long charm to protect a baby from evil spirits.

In personal as well as in the symbolic life of the spirit, the wail and the incantation were required to bring about the rebirth after death. A funeral was a great religious ceremony at which women, whose particular and unique function was mourning, always participated. They followed the bier in a procession, throwing ashes on their heads, waving green branches, scratching their cheeks, holding tear cups to their eyes, and screaming themselves hoarse. The wailers were sometimes members of the family, but they could also be professionals who made wailing a specialty distinct from the musical lament or dirge.

Often the dead body was borne on a barge across the Nile, followed by other barges carrying wailers and choirs of women singers. Statuettes of Isis and Nephthys, goddess composers of both wails and laments, might be placed at one end of the boat and surrounded by women performing the rite of wailing. At the other end another group of women led by a choir mistress might officiate as singers. (See Plate 28.)

At home, the funeral feast was accompanied by music. Women played the lyre and the flute, beat their drums, and clapped their hands to the rhythm of songs invoking the blessing of a goddess whose function it was to receive the dead. "Put balsam in the locks of Ma'et; for health and life are with her. . . ." (See Plate 29.)

In old Egypt both the love lyric and the song-story reached a high point of development. There is a flower song in one of the famous collections similar in imagery to other women's flower songs in all parts of the world. A maiden is weaving a wreath. Each flower she adds reminds her of her love:

> Blush roses are in it [the wreath], one blushes before thee—
> My life depends upon hearing thee.
> Whenever I see thee, it is better to me than food or drink.[9]

Did not some woman there use her musical talent to express her personal emotions and to compose "the beautiful gladsome songs of thy sister whom thy heart loves"?[10] Penthelia, we know, was one who described in song and story the events of the Trojan wars. Her technique is said to have inspired Homer, or other Greek bards, to imitate her treatment of this epic material.

As a priestess of the god Phtha, Penthelia may be regarded as a symbol of the woman who was both a religious official and an enter-tainer. She was only one of many Egyptian women musicians trained for service in the temples who was also expected to use music upon other occasions than the temple ceremony. The large groups of women living in the palaces danced, played, and sang at banquets and other entertainments, employing the same musical ideas and idiom that were appropriate to the rituals. A certain Rahonem was at one time the chief woman manager of the lesser wives, and in her capacity as directress of the female players of the tabour (drum) and of the female singers, had the same title as that given to the priestess-musician.

The princess-musicians were assisted by girls drawn from social classes beneath the rank of royalty and trained in regular music schools. Many pictures show graceful dancers and instrumentalists playing lyres, flutes, and drums in combination. During the Eight-eenth Dynasty these professional women musicians competed suc-cessfully with the blind harpers. In singing, the trained musicians had an undeniable advantage over men. Their voices, believed to be so potent in affecting spirits, combined also the clarity and flexibility for making subtle and delicate melodic variations. Ideals in religion and art converged to bring the woman musician forward in a man-ner unparalleled in the modern world where women and music both have different values.

Women's association with music in Egypt reached a brilliant climax in the Eighteenth Dynasty and continued to be a vital one until the priests converted religion into an organized system of sor-cery from which all but they were excluded. Women's music can be traced back to the earliest days of Egyptian history. In the beginning it was chiefly dancing and singing, especially lamenting, in which they excelled. The oldest goddesses symbolized these early women musicians. In instrumental music women apparently did not partici-pate extensively until about 2700 B.C., after the passing of the Old Empire. Men are depicted as the usual performers on instruments. Some kind of a taboo evidently existed preventing women from be-ing trained in a field in which they later showed so much proficiency. Significantly, the oldest goddesses hold the sistrum but not other instruments. If this negative reflection of women's musical activities has verity, so then must the positive reflection be true to life. And the predominant part taken by these old goddesses over gods in dance and song strongly indicates that real women, whose interests and activities became integrated into divine characters, were in fact leaders in ritual and in music.

4.

Simultaneously with Egypt, peoples of the Near East, allied to the Jews in language, customs, ideas, and physical type, were building another great civilization in the low flat land between the Tigris and Euphrates Rivers. The most southern part of this region, where the rivers come down to the Persian Gulf, was called Chaldea. The northern section, composed of the lower slopes and valleys of the high mountains whence the rivers came, was called Assyria. The great central area—lying low and flat between the rivers—was called Babylonia and was dominated by its great city, Babylon, whose ruins are about seventy miles south of the medieval and modern city of Bagdad. The three sections of this great region are referred to together as Sumer.

The life of Babylonia was the life of merchants and small farmers, busy, prosperous, with widespread education and general comfort and luxury in the arrangements for daily living. It was regulated by an elaborate system of law that guaranteed justice and, in general, favored women and especially mothers. For example, if a free woman married a slave, her children were guaranteed to her and could not be made slaves by the father's master.

Almost everybody in Babylon, both men and women, learned to read. Writing was done with a pointed stylus on tablets of wet clay and baked. Women even had the first woman's college mentioned in history. In the district of Cappadocia, tablets have been found that mention a lady's college in a "women's city." The studies appear to have been arts, letters, and crafts.

As in Egypt, princesses were priestesses and women carried out religious rituals with music and incantations in which the wail was made the basis of a great variety of music. Both men and women played instruments and gave the chants. In Akkadian, the language of north Babylonia, the word for the liturgical psalmist and chanter was *zammertu*, of the feminine gender. Convents of women religious officials called "virgins" were attached to the temples. Though said to be vowed to chastity, actually, under Babylonian law, they were allowed to marry. They were not supposed to have children of their own but might give their husbands a concubine, whose children were regarded as their own. Possibly there is some misunderstanding of the various laws regulating the women religious officials who had a high status and many prerogatives. Possibly the word virgin as applied to these married priestesses means only that they were expected to be persons of decorum or good character. The statement that they were to have no children but might give their husbands a concubine whose children were to be regarded as their own means merely that their duties to the temple must be set above those to their home. In compensation for which they might very properly get another woman to manage their households!

Temples were great storehouses of surplus products under the administration of the state, for which people in privation might make application. A tenth or tithe of all products was contributed to the temple—whence comes the practice of tithing in the Jewish and Christian churches. A similar plan of making the temple the storehouse of surpluses to help the people in famines was followed in early Persia. It seems a natural expression of a mother's forethought.

In the temples there was an elaborate music by women, under the direction of the queen and princesses as priestesses. Queen Shu-bad of Ur made music on harp and tambourine with her ladies in waiting or with professional musicians. In her society, too, the word *nartu,* meaning "chanter," is feminine. Lipushiau, the granddaughter of King Naram-Sin, was appointed player of the *balag-di* drum in the moon god's temple at Ur. This drum was used not only for the liturgy but at feasts. Its other name, *balag-lul,* has a connection with singing. We can fancy this girl of 2380 B.C. drumming and making incantations to hasten the rebirth of the moon and then dancing and singing with her companions in the palace.

In Ishtar's temple at Erech, troops of dancing priestesses chanted their laments in a dialect used only when a female deity was supposed to be reciting. Although the word "wailing" is repeated in every line, the tradition of Ishtar as "She of the Beautiful Voice" and other references to "sacred music" point to some form of singing accompanying the utilitarian magic of the wail. Choral dancing in connection with national victory or defeat was a widespread custom. When the Sumerians and Akkadians were being oppressed by their Gutian conquerors during the third millennium B.C., the women of several towns assembled to mourn their fate. Dividing into two choruses, they gave the lament antiphonally, each group singing, in alternation, appropriate verses. At a much later date a document from Babylonia records that a certain group of women musicians were to assist in the celebration for a victorious army. Such performances, of which many other examples could be given, were by no means an impromptu or an individual expression of emotion but an organized, studied affair demanded by public opinion.

The tendency of all this religious and musical ritual under the leadership of singing women in Babylonia was toward an intellectual and monotheistic religion that had an influence for many centuries over religious thought. But the soul of the universe, as the Babylonians saw it, was not the male warrior god on which the monotheistic imagination of other near-by Semites, the Jews, later fastened, but was instead an all-encompassing mother principle, generally personified as Ishtar. Ishtar was Life—the teeming life of the rich Babylonian plain. She was in the waving grain, in the figs and the olive trees, in the fat cattle and sheep, in the inexhaustible waters from the high mountains that watered the garden lands the Sumerians had made for themselves. She was in the bright fostering sun by day and the moon and stars by night. Ishtar was not a goddess like the other gods and goddesses of Babylonia. She was something above and behind them, the ultimate explanation, universal being, life itself.

Between the superhuman woman-being and earthly men and women the imagination of the Babylonians created not only a pantheon of deities, but a host of intermediary spirits. Spirits were everywhere. The unseen world was full of imagined beings, both female and male, local and specialized representatives of the ultimate life, who might be influenced by the singing magic or incantations. Women had their special wisdom, which was revered by men. The oracles at Arbela were always regarded as being divinely inspired. And always the singing women continued to invoke the fertile power of Ishtar. If her power appeared to fail them, they created lamentations that sometimes have great poetic beauty and remind us of many passages in the Bible. The intention of these, as in all wail songs of women, is to invoke the rebirth.

The wailing is for the plants, the first lament is, "they grow not."
The wailing is for the barley; the ears grow not,
For the habitations and the flocks it is, they produce not.

For the perishing wedded ones, for perishing children it is: the dark-headed people create not. The wailing is for the great river: it brings the flood no more.

. . .

The wailing is for the forests; the tamarisks grow not.

. . .

The wailing is for the garden store-house; honey and wine are produced not.

. . .

The wailing is for the palace; life unto distant days is not.[11]

5.

The mountainous island of Crete, only a hundred and fifty miles long and from seven to thirty-five miles wide, is a small place to have been the seat of a great civilization. Though its lower valleys are well-watered and fertile, the land growing lemons, oranges, pears, grapes, and olives to perfection, it could hardly have sustained a large number of people. But, from about 3000 to 1200 B.C., the Cretans traded far and wide with people on the shores and other islands of the Mediterranean Sea. They seem to have made these contacts without much fighting. Few civilizations of which we have record are so unmilitary or have lasted so long. The culture was, in every way, an example of a beneficent type of matriarchy, with women as goddess-priestess-musicians.

The immense and remarkable remains of its "hundred cities" reveal that artistic and engineering talent were devoted, not to temples and tombs, but to details of household life. In the palace at Knossus, there was plumbing such as Europe did not know until the nineteenth century. The town of Knossus was crossed by a well-paved street with a stone sewer and was flanked with fine private homes. The frescoed walls show women dancers and gymnasts, as well as priestesses in costumes similar to those in the rock paintings of Spain. (See Plate 37.) Yet in other pictures, the clothes are surprisingly modern. In their flounced skirts, trim waists, and decorative sleeves, these Cretan women seem to move and sing. No other ancient paintings are as lifelike.

Crete, like Egypt and Sumer, illustrates the principle that in that period of history, women were the inspirers and the chief ministrants of spiritual life. Gods were rare and inconspicuous, goddesses numerous and important. This society, which has left such charming records of polished and refined daily living, shared with some African tribes (especially the Bantu) many of the regular female symbols. Among these, either wholly female or combining female and male characteristics, were the moon, the double axe, pillars, rocks, trees, flowers, shells, snakes, and birds.

In the service of the deities and other symbols of life, priestesses predominated. Many frescoes depict women conducting a sacrifice attended by men porters. When the men attendants carried musical instruments, they dressed like women. When youths joined a choir, they were led by a priestess and imitated the dress of maidens, as if to deceive the spirits into believing them members of the stronger spiritual sex. (See Plate 32.)

The spiritual superiority of women was manifested also in the small images of musicians made for the purpose of accompanying the dead in their graves. The manufacture of these figurines—invariably feminine—was a regular industry, especially in the nearby Cyclades Islands.

It is a striking fact that nothing remains of an overemphasis in the glory of man as king, priest, or husband. Polygamy evidently had no vogue in Crete. Monogamous marriage was the custom. In a betrothal scene, depicted on an ivory cylinder near Knossus, the man and the woman, both the same height, raise their right arms for a handclasp. They stand as equals.

The presence of small chapels in the women's quarters of the palace indicates that informal and formal rites were indistinguishable. The queen—high priestess—probably burnt her incense, poured out holy water, lit her torches, and arranged her flowers in vases of her own making on her domestic altar. Being both a normal mother and a representative of a goddess, such a worshiper would repeat at home her incantations for protecting her family and for controlling spirits.

Girls had their swings hanging between pillars topped by the sacred doves, symbols of love and fertility. At their first pregnancy, they may have been called to their rites by a mother blowing a seashell trumpet as girls today in South Sea islands are summoned by the priestess in charge. (See Plate 36.) When rain was needed, women sprang in ecstatic motion around the great rock which represented Rhea, spirit of flowing water and goddess of the dance. The fame of such dancers spread far beyond the borders of their own land and long after their own time. Sappho sang: "Thus of old did the dainty feet of Cretan maidens dance pat to the music beside some lovely altar, pressing the soft smooth bloom of the grass." [12] Public religious festivals were probably staged out-of-doors in an open stadium. Plate 30 shows a ceremony conducted by priestesses and attended by a large assembly of women and men. The object of adoration is unfortunately missing, but Sir Arthur Evans suggests that it may have been the day-spring from on high in the shape of a tiny goddess. (See Plate 31.) One can imagine hearing the voices of the priestess-musicians chanting hymns, songs of praise, laments, and joyful songs of the birth. Hymnos, paen, elegoes, and dithyrambos are Greek terms for poetic forms which, with the skillful use of melodic norms, derived from Crete.

This choral dance on the "Isle of Women" seems to be the forerunner of the Greek tragedies in which men dressed as women and acted the part of women characters. What would give clearer evidence of the fact that men first imitated, and then developed for a purpose of their own, rites which had been invented and utilized for centuries by women in the mother's religion?

6.

No names of individual creative musicians have survived from those far-off times. There is no way of knowing whether men or women excelled in the invention of dances and music. But women's relation to music and to a religion, based on the sense of the glory and power of woman's function as life bearer, was very different from that of the woman of today, outwardly free but spiritually devitalized, with no faith in her womanhood to inspire her to song.

All these ancient religions were based on the primitive woman's grand idea that she who gives birth can invoke the rebirth—that, as mother, she has authority over life and death. And this authority she exercised by making music. The intimate relation in ancient societies between goddess, queen, priestess, and ordinary woman meant that the collective body of women was drawn into a musical life that had its origin in connection with institutions and occasions planned in previous centuries by women themselves. It meant that the woman with creative musical imagination had behind her a long tradition of capability on the part of women and that she started composing on an already high plateau of experience and achievement.

Occasions for the development of musical talent had already been formalized in the regular events of living—in the birth of a baby, rebirth at adolescence, marriage, death, and springtide, in the work of feeding, clothing, and manufacturing needed articles, in caring for children, and in amusement. All the ancients recognized and valued woman's bond with the life force. There was no denial of the imaginative faculty. Institutions existed for the purpose of directing her beneficent power into the proper channels. Music was regarded as a direct extension of the functions of women. As in primitive tribes, the barriers between women and music were merely local limitations upon specific occasions when women were expected to function as musicians. As long as there were goddesses, queens, and priestesses, as long as there were women leaders holding positions of responsibility in musical life, women were adapting and arranging the inherited songs and dances, or creating variations on them for new occasions. And they were doing this on their own inspiration, in the proud consciousness that, as women and mothers, they sang with voices that the great powers of life would be bound to heed.

CHAPTER VII

THE LYRIC POETESS

1.

SOME time between 2000 B.C. and 1000 B.C. our modern world began. For on the great plains of Russia, north of the Black Sea and the Caspian, another people—the Aryans—began stirring. During the next centuries they moved outward in all directions, traveling great distances, riding on horses, and driving their cattle before them. They went down into India, pushed back the older Dravidians into southern India, took over the north of India, and began to tell their own story in the *Rig-Veda*. They came down into the Near East and established Persia, whose present name, Iran, means Aryan. They spread westward into Europe and gave their language and customs to whoever was living there at the time when they arrived. Above all, they took over, one after another, the isles and peninsulas of the eastern Mediterranean and put themselves to school amidst the Cretans, choosing and modifying and usually simplifying the charming civilization they found there. Greek civilization did not originate as a single country or culture. It began among little groups of rather rude, hardy people who settled in amidst the decaying luxury and splendor of richer and brighter days, and who in their own plain way civilized themselves by borrowing from their betters.

The one bond among these early Greeks was that they spoke the same language. This was a bond, more or less, among all Aryan peoples, from the misty shores of Ireland to the sunburned banks of the Ganges. This was and is the only bond. Aryan does not refer to a race or a color of skin. It refers only to a kind of language. An early Chinese writer who saw these Aryans in India mentioned their distinctive appearance, however, as well as their widespread language

87

and their attitude to women. "From Wan westward to An-si the languages of the people, though differing slightly from one another are generally similar so that they may understand one another when conversing. All these people have deep eyes and a rich growth of beard. They hold their women in high honor, for whatever a woman says, her husband invariably agrees to it." [1]

Wherever people speak the same language, they tend to have common ideas and social attitudes. The first of the Aryans to write down their ideas about life were those in India. In the *Rig-Veda*, written perhaps about 1200 B.C., there are references to women and to their authority in religion, music, and social life. "From of old comes the wife to the public sacrifice and to the festive gathering; as orderer of the sacrifice comes the noble woman attended by men." [2] This record from the sacred books indicates that the wife was essential to the ceremony.

An especially beautiful service was one performed at the hearth-altar. "O gods," says the *Rig-Veda*, "the married couple, who together intend to present to you libations—who together come on the grass to place there the sacred food—[grant that] this couple, surrounded by little children and growing sons and daughters, pass a happy life. . . ." [3]

At the marriage ceremony, the company chanted hymns to Agni, the fire god, invoking perfection of the well-knit bond between husband and wife. One such hymn, in which only feminine adjectives appear, has been ascribed to the poetess-musician Visvavara, a member of the priestly family of Atreya.

> Show thyself strong for mighty bliss, O Agni,
>
> .   .   .
>
> And overcome the might of those who hate us! [4]

With these Aryan people, marriage ensured the mother and her children protection from the native enemy hordes but apparently did not limit her personal liberty beyond the natural prescriptions of physiological laws or pervert the relationship into a degradation of woman's natural powers. In ancient India a boy was thought to be blessed eightfold if his mother presided at his initiation into manhood. Institutions through which woman's authority in matters of rebirth rituals could be maintained continued to hold people's respect.

As Pandy says to his wife, Kunty, in the Indian epic, the Mahab-

34. Raishallala of the Tuareg tribe of northern Africa, photographed in front of her tent, is a modern example of the ancient Mediterranean poetess-musician. (See page 72.)

35, 36, 37. Women musicians of ancient Egypt and Crete.
(See pages 75, 83, and 84.)

38. On a small bas-relief from ancient Greece, the goddess Eileithyia protects the mother in childbirth. (See page 96.)

39. In ancient Greece, the swing festival was a woman's rite associated with the rhythm of life. (See page 100.)

40, 41, 42. Greek artists often decorated their pottery with representations of women working, rejoicing at weddings, and mourning at funerals. (See pages 98, 99, and 101.)

From A. Furtwängler. Griechische Vasenmalerei

43. Greek girls learned their religious dances from women musicians. (See page 103.)

Courtesy of G. Routledge & Sons, Ltd.

44. Sappho, honored by her pupils, sang, "Mark me, the after days shall see, those that will still remember me." (See page 107.)

harata, which reflects the life of a later day, "I shall tell thee about the practice of old indicated by illustrious Rishis fully acquainted with every rule of morality. O, thou handsome of face and sweet smiles, women were not formerly immured in houses and dependent upon husbands and relatives. They used to go about freely enjoying themselves as best they pleased." [5]

The next records we have of the way the early Aryans felt are the poems of Homer, which began to be sung (perhaps as early as 1000 B.C.) all up and down the islands of the Aegean, and the shores of Greece and Asia Minor, where the Greeks were settling. All these Greeks traced their ancestry to Helen, the daughter of the moon. The hero of one of the two great Homeric poems, the Iliad, is Achilles, grandson of the lunar goddess Doris, the Engenderer. Doris had fifty daughters known as the Nereids. One of them, "silver-slippered Thetis," was the mother of Achilles.

These early Greek stories concern the kidnaping of their beautiful Helen by the Trojans, also Aryans, who carried her away to Asia, and the attempts of the kings of Argos and Mycenae and innumerable heroes, sons of goddesses, to get her back. Woman is such an all-pervading, all-protecting spirit in the Odyssey, the other great Homeric epic, that it is not unlikely that the poem was fashioned by weaving together lays earlier composed and sung by women.

2.

Throughout Greek history until about 400 B.C., when the drama began to absorb public interest and the theater usurped the mimetic rite, singing, dancing, and playing on instruments had the same significance and the same utility that they have today for our primitive and peasant contemporaries. Music was deemed by them a thing divine, the breath of life, a tremendous power for influencing the thought and actions of people, for controlling nature and supernatural beings.

Like other ancient peoples, the Greeks placed a high value on the art of the dance, which they regarded, like swinging, as a means for keeping in the flow of life and for ensuring equilibrium to the soul. Many of the dance movements had come from magic gestures intended to awaken life. The high leap and the wide sweep of the leg won immortality for the dead or made the corn grow tall. Scooping imaginary dewdrops with the hands, arching arms like the moon were techniques to stimulate growth. Holding hands and forming a circle conveyed the strength of the group to each individual.

With the art of manufacturing musical instruments capable of fine gradations of tone still in its infancy, the voice was naturally the favorite medium for musical expression. In the golden ages of Egypt and Crete, emphasis was placed upon melody—a development that the Greeks later carried far toward perfection. But behind this art was practical magic, revealed by words in several of the ancient Aryan languages besides Greek. In Sanskrit, for instance, the word *mantra,* which means a verse of praise to a deity, comes also to mean a magical invocation to compel that higher power to grant some human appeal. The old Indians had charms known as *rāga* and *rāginī,* Aryan words that have survived in the Lithuanian language as *ragana,* meaning one who makes magic formulas or incantations. In Latin, the words *carmen* and *ode* both have the double meaning of "song" and "charm."

Music, indeed, to the Indians of former days, was regarded as being conformable to cosmic laws when it was brought into juxtaposition with certain seasons and hours. Were every rule about the performance of music strictly obeyed, the six male *rāga* tunes and the thirty female *rāginīs* were then considered capable of producing some desired effect. Should they be used in defiance of tradition, a calamity, such as the turning of day into night, might ensue. (See Plate 45.)

In Greece, the conception of the universal life force operating through music was given a beautiful expression by the fifth century B.C. philosopher Pythagoras and his wife Theano, a poetess-musician. They taught that the spheres and the stars of heaven move to music in an eternal song and dance. And so they organized rites for their followers, to the end that each person, by taking part in the music and the dance, might achieve an inner harmony of spirit.

Later Greek educators and philosophers employed the various musical "modes" which had developed through centuries of musical experience to induce a state of mind or "mood." A certain arrangement of tones in a scale was believed to be capable of inspiring soldiers with courage; another was used to inspire worshipers with reverence; still another stimulated passion. Plato later proposed that music for young people should be limited to those modes that would strengthen their characters. He desired to imitate the Egyptians in the creation of melodies that had the capability of calming human passions and purging the soul. The seriousness with which he advanced his theory shows that the most highly educated men believed in the *affective* power of music and of music as an accompaniment to the other arts. Of such social and religious uses for music, professionalism and the training of professional performers of music were by-products. For many centuries the important music of that great Greek culture remained in its primitive milieu—in the religious rite, for the purpose of placing the worshipers in accord with the life force; in the home, for work, recreation, and magic; at the banquet and formal social gatherings, for entertainment. Consequently in early Greece women were at the center of these three types of music. They danced, sang, and played instruments, especially flutes and cymbals and drums. From childhood to the grave, at home, in small group gatherings, and in formal public ceremonials, early Greek women had opportunity and occasion to use music, and incentive to compose it. The result of such a setting was a rich musical experience for women in general and a great wealth of songs composed for women and by women.

Throughout the period of ancient times until the Christian Era, and even long after, the Greeks like other ancient creators of music usually followed the primitive custom of associating their songs, dances, and instrumental playing with a specific occasion and purpose. Musical art reached its climax when it enhanced the emotional value of some event—a victory over enemy armies, defeat in battle, a wedding, a funeral, a religious festival, a public or private entertainment. The same musical idiom served for all occasions and purposes; one cannot tell from the picture whether a religious rite is being celebrated or whether an entertainment is being staged. This is because the function of music had not changed since the most primitive times. People believed that music was for the purpose of heightening emotional reactions. No matter what the occasion, the artist employed the same techniques.

3.

As in all goddess-worshiping cultures, priestesses in Greece were valued and respected members of their communities. They usually came from noble families and held their offices by hereditary right. Priestesses were assisted in their duties by the so-called *hierai*, sacred women, and the girl choristers. These remained an integral part of the religious and musical life of Greece until long after the beginning of the Christian Era. Members of the choir received training in their youth for the proper performance of the dances and religious songs, often spending the year before marriage within the precincts of a temple under the guidance of a priestess.

Priestesses assembled in societies or hierarchies. Some of the best known were the Oleiai of Orchomenos, the Dysmainai of Mount Taygetos, and the Dionysiades of Sparta. Most renowned of all were the Thyiades, a society whose origin is shrouded in the mists of antiquity. Its members claimed descent from Ino, mother of the Danoi, who, legend tells, brought women's rites from Egypt to Greece. Ino herself was the Horned Cow, like the crescent moon. The Thyiades had colleges in several different places, notably Elis, Pisatis, Sparta, and Delphi. They served both Hera and Dionysos; and when celebrating rites for the rebirth of Dionysos, they were led by the mythical mother of Dionysos, Semele. Though Dionysos was the god of wine and later was worshiped by drunken votaries, his rites in Crete and old Greece were not orgiastic in the sense of intoxication from drink. The women who belonged to these important religious institutions sang their hymns and danced their dances in sobriety. Their ecstasy was a ritual, performed in imitation of the maenads of immemorial tradition and for the same immemorial reason—to become one with the rhythm of all life. (See Plate 33.)

The cult of Dionysos, which was widely and enthusiastically accepted throughout the classical world in the pre-Christian centuries, represented a religious idea that seems to have had an extraordinary popular appeal—the idea that a woman might bear a child without the interposition of a human father, in ecstatic union with a god. This child might be a son or a daughter, and in some cases the divine infant was thought of as of both sexes. But whether son or daughter, the young divinity born like a human baby, nurtured at a human mother's breast, growing up as a human being, beautiful and beloved, demonstrated that through the woman's body alone, with no help from the human male, the universal life force might be incarnated in a young being who was both human and divine. This idea, which appears in various forms in Greek mythology, was best represented by the young god Dionysos, son of Semele and Zeus.

It is important to emphasize the fact that in the earliest times all Dionysiac cults were exclusively women's cults and that they came from the Cretan culture where only women were the priestesses. The song of the birth (dithyramb) was the song of the mothers, and by tradition the women choirs of the tribe of Akamantis had used the primitive cry of joy—alleluia. Priestesses of Elis, probably the distinguished women who belonged to the college of the Thyiades priesthood, sang the oldest dithyramb preserved in Greek literature:

> In springtime, O Dionysos,
> To thy holy temple come,
> To Elis with thy Graces,
> Rushing with thy bull-foot, come,
> Noble Bull, noble Bull! [6]

From these symbolic mothers singing their dithyramb invoking the divine child to birth, back to the midwife chanting her incantations to hasten the arrival of the human child, we see the extraordinary continuity of Greek ritualistic practice, the carry-over of personal experience to group emotional expression.

The most usual name for the worshipers of Dionysos was the Bacchae or the bacchantes. Both words mean "the mothers." With Dionysos were associated also ancient mythical women called maenads. We know much about these singing, dancing societies of women and their secret rites in the mountains. For in a later century an inquiring and sensitive man named Euripides happened to escape from the rather conceited circles of the male intelligentsia of Athens in his day and to catch a glimpse of them. He was profoundly stirred and wrote a beautiful choral drama, *The Bacchae* (or *The Mothers*), about them. Had Euripides known more about the primitive origins of his own civilization, he might have avoided a groping indefiniteness in his beautiful verse. But he believed, in his poet's soul, that these women, with their ringing cry, "Oh, wild white maids, to the hills, to the hills!" [7] had something men might well try to understand.

Their rites, he thought, came from Crete, and he represented the Bacchae as singing:

> "For thee of old some crested Corybant
> First woke in Cretan air
> The wild orb of our orgies,
> Our Timbrel; and thy gorges
> Rang with this strain; and blended Phrygian chant
> And sweet keen pipes were there.

"But the Timbrel, the Timbrel was another's,
And away to Mother Rhea it must wend;
And to our holy singing from the Mothers
The mad Satyrs carried it, to blend
In the dancing and the cheer
Of our third and perfect year." [8]

Casting an interested masculine eye over their attire, but not apparently aware of the age-old meaning of their symbols, Euripides noted that the Bacchae wore long white dresses and had fawn skins flung over their shoulders, and that some of them carried wands with serpents wound around them. "The Songs of Serpents sound in the mazes of their hair." [9] Perhaps he had never heard that the snake is from immemorial time the symbol of rebirth. All the maidens carried oak wands wreathed in ivy. Most of them had ivy wound in their hair. They had outposts to warn all onlookers away. A maiden went ahead of the procession chanting:

"Who lingers in the road? Who espies us?
He shall hide him in his house nor be bold.
Let the heart keep silence that defies us;
For I sing this day to Dionysos
The song that is appointed from of old." [10]

And when the women, seeking the still dell of the Muses, had climbed far into the hills (as primitive women in Africa do to this day), a shepherd saw them in the dawn, sleeping after their night-long songs and incantations.

"Our herded kine were moving in the dawn
Up to the peaks, the greyest, coldest time,
When the first rays steal earthward, and the rime
Yields, when I saw three bands of them. The one
Autonoe led, one Ino, one thine own
Mother, Agave. There beneath the trees
Sleeping they lay, like wild things flung at ease
In the forests; one half sinking on a bed
Of deep pine greenery; one with careless head
Amid the fallen oak leaves; all most cold
In purity—not as thy tale was told
Of wine-cups and wild music and the chase
For love amid the forest's loneliness." [11]

While there were a few mysteries in which men and women jointly participated, most of the secret rites were conducted by women alone, and only by initiated women. Those that concern women's mysteries have never been fully understood since their meaning was not disclosed to any uninitiated person. The whole subject of the women's hierarchies—their secrecy, their mythical association with goddesses and with the moon—takes us back into the farthest realm of primitive times and shows the force of those old beliefs even among people as highly educated as the Greeks.

4.

The expression of religious feeling by means of rites was an integral part of Greek daily life. The Greeks had inherited belief in the power of magic, and they placated their numerous deities at every turn—in their homes, at wayside shrines, in sacred groves and caves, and later with formal ceremonies in the great temples of the classical age. Before a meal a Greek family would place on its hearth a few bits of food in offering to Hestia, goddess of the hearth, and would pour a few drops of unmixed wine on the floor to placate the good daemon of the house. Women made obeisance to Eileithyia and to Hekate, goddesses of life and death, at shrines erected at the thresholds of their homes. In his "Ode to Theron," Pindar tells of the maidens who danced and sang before his door through the night.

Divine protection was particularly required for the special events in human life—for birth, presentation of the child to society and to the spirits, puberty, marriage, and death—and for the normal changes of nature—the birth and decay of vegetation. In the main, Greek religious rites centered around these rhythmical crises. The character of the rites varied all the way from simple house cult practices of primitive times to elaborate festivals involving many people and lasting for days.

The most striking aspect of Greek religious practice is the continuity of its expression—the constant carry-over from the real to the ideal; from actual experience to a deity who symbolized the experience. To women, this constant carry-over was extraordinarily important. All their activities, all their physiological crises had feminine impersonations to whom they could voice their needs. In these symbols women projected their own strength and capabilities, their own value in the life scheme. In the worship of the goddesses, women had opportunity and compulsion to express with ritual and music their own deep emotions, their own creative urges. Help for a woman in childbirth, for example, was not confined to incantations sung by a midwife to ease and speed her actual labor. In congregation, at shrines—such as the shrine at Olympia that Eileithyia, goddess of childbirth, shared with the snake-child Sosipolis—women sang formal hymns to their protectress. At the great festival of the Thesmophoria, sacred to married women, it was customary on the third day for the women votaries to sing a hymn of invocation to Artemis Kalligenia, or Prothyraia, to her who would grant an easy birth to mothers. (See Plate 38.)

To Artemis Prothyraia

Hear me, O most majestic goddess, spirit of the many names,
Deliveress from the pangs of birth, sweet presence to those in travail,
Savioress of women, you who alone love children, goddess of the
    gentle mind,
Giver of a birth that is rapid, deliveress from mortal sorrows,
Prothyraia, you who are before the Door!
Who hold the keys, beautiful to meet, kind to all,
    who love to feed and keep animals,
Of the homes of all you are mistress, you rejoice in the gladness of
    feasts,
Loosener of girdles, invisible, yet manifest by your works to all!
Through sympathy you suffer along with women in travail,
And with those who bring forth easily you rejoice,
Ilithyia, goddess of childbirth, releaser from the throes none can
    escape!
On you alone they call in travail, O resting-place of the soul,
For in you the pains of childbirth are forgotten.
Artemis Ilithyia, and Prothyraia, hallowed in beauty,
Hear, blessed one! Give the fruit of seed, coming as a deliveress,
And saving us, even as you were born eternal Savioress of all! [12]

The woman's singing magic of birth and rebirth was used in the various rites of the life cycle as it still is among primitive peoples. At puberty, Greek girls were inducted into maturity with various minutiae of ceremony. As with primitive tribes, flowers, the holy bath, games, foot races, festivals at the new moon, and always dancing and singing were characteristic features of these ceremonials. For example, girl initiates serving Hera, in whose cult flowers were always used, would gather spring blossoms and twine them around a statue of the goddess as they danced to the music of flutes and invoked the holy one in song. In ceremonies of Artemis at Sicyon, where the Crete-inherited feminine influence was especially strong, a statue of the goddess was annually carried down to the sea and dipped into the water for the sacred bath. The most beautiful girl initiate was chosen to impersonate the goddess, and a choir of dancing and singing girls led the procession to the sea. In the rear followed a choir of boys, also dancing and singing. These boys probably represent a relatively late addition to a ritual in which originally only women and girls took part. The great festival of the Heraea, held under the direction of the Thyiades in the month of Parthenos, when the moon was new, was also a puberty rite, a festival of games for girls like the Olympic games for boys, and probably of older origin. The music for the Heraea was made by the Thyiades. Under their organization and leadership, two choirs of sixteen women sang the sacred hymns.

Little is known of the Heraea, but it is not difficult to guess the character of the rites or to infer the leadership of women. These women's rites are alike the world over. Among the Tusayan Indians in New Mexico, for example, the La-la-konta Festival lasts for ten days and has a deep religious significance for the whole tribe. Its chief purpose is to induce the germination of seeds. The girls run a race, a common practice at puberty rites and certainly a feature of the Heraea. There is a procession to the spring—water is always the source of life—and a dance. The priestesses hold their office by heredity. After ceremonially calling the women together at the shrine, they lead them in wonderful choral singing. As we have seen in many places in the primitive world, as well as in Egypt, the priestess is also musician. Undoubtedly in Greece, women with the same status also composed their own music for their own rites.

Marriage rites in Greece, like those of puberty, were rites of transition from one state of life to another, celebrated both at real and at symbolic marriages. Real weddings usually took place just before full moon. Before the ceremony, sacrifices to the goddesses were made and the bride was given her sacramental bath. At the festivities the bride was veiled to signify rebirth from a symbolic womb and also to signify dedication to her new life. The two mothers lit the torches that symbolized the light of the life-giving moon. Accompanied by flute players, the wedding procession marched to the

bridegroom's house. The wedding feast was the ideal time for felicita-
tions. (See Plate 41.)

Bridesmaids greeted the bridegroom:

> "Raise high the roof-beam, carpenters,
>   Hymenaeus!
> Like Ares comes the bridegroom,
>   Hymenaeus!
> Taller far than a tall man,
>   Hymenaeus!" [13]

The hymn-call was to bring forth the daemons of fertility. It was always shouted at weddings as a kind of good-luck motto by the
friends of the bride and groom. Bridesmaids at a Greek wedding always lamented the passing of the bride's girlhood. In Sappho's words
they sang:

> "Maidenhood, maidenhood, whither art thou gone from me?
> Never again will I come to thee, never again." [14]

Then groomsmen would praise the bride: "O fair, O lovely!" and the
wedding guests would praise the bridal pair:

> "Hail, bride!
> Noble bridegroom!
> All hail!" [15]

It was the bridesmaids' duty and pleasure to prepare the bridal
bed in a bower garlanded with flowers, and to conduct the bride to
it. The epithalamium, accompanied by dancing, was sung outside
of the bridal chamber at night by bridesmaids and youths. At dawn
came the last benediction of the friends:

> "Farewell the bride,
> Farewell the bridegroom." [16]

In temples and at festivals, sacred marriages, symbolic of the union
of the sexes, were performed on many occasions, often with other
rebirth rites. At the Heraea festival, for example, the girl victorious
in the foot races, olive-crowned, would be married symbolically to
the boy winner of the Olympic games. At the rites of Dionysos in

Athens the wife of the second archon officiated regularly as bride to a symbolic Dionysos. Sometimes, as in the cult of Hera at Samos, the rites of the sacred marriage were performed without men, but they were never performed without women—a fact that clearly suggests a feminine origin of the marriage rite as a *"rite de passage"* for a woman about to enter a new state of life. In Greek religion the rites of the sacred marriage and of the birth of the holy child or of some symbol of the rebirth were indissoluble and represented the central mystery of religious ritual.

Greek funeral rites, like other rites of the rebirth, were held for both real and for symbolic deaths. When a person died, the family and the professional women mourners would gather around the bier. It was the business of the professional mourner to give the wailing necessary to hasten the rebirth of the dead soul into the spirit world. The mourner was expected to remain for several days, during which time she sang one dirge after another. A mourner was not worth her pay if she repeated herself. She probably behaved very like the present-day professional singer at funerals in Mykonos. In old Greece the group of family mourners burst out with a refrain. The men exclaimed in their own characteristic fashion and the women gave the *evoe*, "Alleluia," similar to the cry of joy given by priestesses in the bacchanals. Sometimes a flute player, also a woman, accompanied the cortege. There was a great demand for these women artists and they had consequently a strong incentive to create music that would be considered good among professionals. (See Plate 42.)

Part of the funeral ceremony was often conducted very like a drama. The cortege consisted of a chariot, or men, bearing the coffin, of women walking in front, at the sides, and in the rear. It was the custom to display grief. The women beat their breasts, wailed for a time, then walked in silence, then wailed again. When the procession halted, the mourners grouped themselves in dramatic attitudes. Sometimes there would be formal choirs. Following a very old custom, the people of Megara used to send fifty maidens and fifty youths to Corinth whenever a death occurred in the Bacchiad family. In all types of death ceremonies women played their classic role.

At the symbolic deaths, mourning for the dead vegetation of the year, or for a hero, a heroine, or a god, a goddess took the place of mourning for a real person. During the Thesmophoria, married women stood at the crossroads and lamented in spirit with Demeter, goddess of the grain, who was searching for her lost daughter, Kore.

In the Adonia, women wailed on their housetops for Adonis, a vegetation god. At all the festivals, after the lamenting came the cries of joy in anticipation of the resurrection, be it of nature, the moon, or the deity.

5.

Religious festivals in Greece showed many traces of a matriarchal origin. In the great periodic rites known as the Thargelia for transferring the force behind vegetation to the new harvest, men and women celebrated together, as do those of many primitive tribes in similar fertility festivals. Men and women both joined, too, in those for Adonis as well as in the requiems, from which our idea of All Saints' and All Souls' Days came. Connected with the rites of the Anthesteria were the Eumenides or avengers of a mother's wrongs. Women sang as they walked along carrying flowers and green branches. In Aeschylus' drama *The Eumenides* is a description of what was probably the actual rites:

> Pass to your house thus augustly estated,
> Come, O mysterious maidens, come, offspring of night!
> And silence all for our sacred song.
> Come ye with sacrifice offered, with worship and with rite.

Some festivals celebrated by men were modeled on women's festivals. The Apatouria—Festival of the Same Fathers—was, for example, an adaptation of a far older form, Festival of the Same Mothers.

Many rites of rebirth were practiced by women alone, or with men playing a secondary role. Korythalia was the women's version of the various May-pole dances (*eiresione*). The Aiora, or Swing Festival, was distinctly a women's ritual, bound up with the moon and the rhythm of life. (See Plate 39.) Besides the Heraea, which had the primitive girls' puberty rites in the race at new moon, there were other festivals of Hera. One was the Anthesphoria, celebrated with flutes amidst bowers of greens. Various Artemisia belonged to women. In them the features were processions to a sacred spring, bronze tympani, and laments called *oupingi*. At the Hersephoria the dew-carrying maidens refreshed the bloom of their own youth. The Tithenidia was a festival for the nursing mothers of Sparta, who danced and sang to Artemis as they ate loaves of bread shaped like a woman's breast. Like the Eleusinian mysteries, the Thesmophoria concerned agricultural magic—woman's ancient prerogative. It was conducted by married women.

Many festivals of Dionysos belonged to women originally, as well as the Adonia, in which Aphrodite's son, or lover, was first mourned for as dead and then rejoiced over as resurrected. Three festivals made up the Ennateric group. The second of this group was the Herois, in which the women invoked Semele, mother of Dionysos, and called upon the dead heroines to return and help them in their colossal task of bringing life to the earth. The third was the Charila and involved carrying out death, preparing for new life. At Orchomenos, where the Thyiades had one of their colleges, the priestesses sang to the Charites, the gift-bringers of plenty.

Greek songs, both religious and occupational, were divided into categories and had generic names. There were songs of winnowing, songs of reaping, mill songs that women sang as they ground grain, songs of the water carriers, and rope songs sung at the well in imitation of the gurgling water. (See Plate 40.)

Nursing mothers had songs of their own—*katabaukaleses*, which means literally to lull to sleep. The bakers sang to Demeter: "Send forth a sheaf, a plenteous sheaf, a sheaf send forth!" [17] (See Plate 16.)

6.

Out of the rich musical life of Greece, with its many opportunities for women to sing and to make music, came a substantial number of poetess-musicians whose fame has carried down to our own day. A Greek compiler lists forty such poetesses by name. These women won numerous prizes in public competitions, had statues erected to them, and some were likened to the Muses by their men competitors. Phantasia, who came to Greece from Memphis, Egypt, in pre-Homeric times, was one of the early story-singers. It was the custom in those days for men and women to gather after supper in the great hall of a dwelling and to amuse themselves by chanting and listening to stories. Phantasia, being a skilled storyteller, like many women in primitive tribes today, entertained her companions with music. She and her friend Themis are reputed to have invented the heroic meter, the hexameter. Certainly they made a compound measure out of two lines of the Linus, that song of lament for Adonis sung by so many choirs of women.

Individual women artists sang laments in public not only in pre-classical and classical Greece but long afterward. In one of his most charming idylls, Theocritus mentioned a skillful singer from Argos who sang in the market place of Syracuse at the festival of Adonis. Two members of the audience, Praxinoe and Gorgo, are speaking: "Silence, Praxinoe! She is preparing to sing the Adonis—the girl of Argos, the skillful singer who carried off the prize of Sperchis, she is preparing to sing the lamentation. She sings, I know well, with talent." The singer modulates the hymn, and Gorgo exclaims: "It is more beautiful than I ever thought; fortunate woman to be so well informed! Altogether fortunate that she sings so softly!" [18] This professional musician was carrying on a custom of immemorial antiquity. She was giving the wail that would hasten the rebirth of Adonis, the god who personified the vegetation of the year. And, according to the way of the woman artist-musician, she had converted the wail into an art form—the musical lament.

Perhaps the two most important categories of women's religious songs were the hymns of invocation composed and sung by the hierarchies of priestesses—notably the Thyiades and the Elean priestesses—and the lyric poems sung by the girl choirs, known as *parthenia* or songs for maidens. The girl choirs were famous for the excellence of their performance. Pindar wrote of them: "Round Parnassus high cliffs, the bright-eyed Delphian maidens enter the fleet chorus and sing a sweet song with clear voices." [19] And Alkman spoke of his delight in the Spartan "maidens of honey voice, so loud and clear." [20]

The songs that the girl choirs sang usually had for theme some myth or legend of god or goddess, hero or heroine. As the girls sang, they would dance and gesticulate and more or less act out the story of the legend. Obviously, this was simply a development of the age-old mimetic rite and a forerunner of the later complicated Greek drama. About the seventh century B.C. a form of choral dance developed, called the *hypercheme,* in which the dancing and gesticulating chorus was reinforced by a stationary group of singers. In this way, more difficult and more complex music could be performed and more attention paid to the melodic element in the music. Favorite subjects for *hyperchemata* were such tales as Bacchylides' myth of Ida and Marpessa, a kind of wedding cantata, or the myth of Theseus' victory over the Minotaur of Crete. In the latter, dancing boys joined with the girls of the dancing chorus. The participation of girl choirs and of actors in this type of ritual dance drama—definite precursor of Greek classical drama, in which only men were allowed to sing or to perform—illustrates the extent to which women took part in the musical life of the preclassical Greeks. (See Plate 43.)

A Greek woman artist—this one distinguished for her singing, her dancing, and her lyric poetry—was Megolastrata of Sparta. Called the beautiful blonde, she led the Spartan girl choirs and composed music for their performances. Unfortunately, not one of her compositions has been preserved, but her fame as a leader and as a composer has come down to us from the seventh century b.c., a time when the girl choirs were especially active and important in Greek life.

Telesilla of Argos was a heroic figure, one of those courageous militant women who through quick decision save their countries in moments of great danger. When the Spartans threatened her city-state, Telesilla is said to have gathered weapons from homes and temples, to have given them to the women of Argos, and to have led them against the enemy. A poetess-musician as well as a warrior, Telesilla is especially famous for her hymns and for her political songs. Only two verses are left from her poetry, a call to maidens, obviously part of a hymn.

Corinna, a poetess-musician of Boetia, was Pindar's teacher and won five times over him in poetic competition. So lovely were her songs that the poet Antipater named her as one of the nine women whom he selected as earthly muses. Corinna's work consisted of epigrams, lyric poems, and choruses for women. Unhappily, only a few fragments of her poetry are extant and none of her melodies. As she herself explained, she sang of native myths and legends, of heroes and especially of heroines—"But I, I am come to sing the prowess of Heroes and Heroines, in fair old-wives' tales for the white-robed daughters of Tanagra!" [21]

Sicyon, a city-state that kept on conspicuously with Cretan customs and in which women played a leading part in both religious and musical life, was the home of the poetess-musician Praxilla. She was famous also for her skolias or table songs—later called drinking songs—sung at banquets, sometimes solo, sometimes in chorus; for her dithyrambs; and for an epic poem entitled "Adonia." Praxilla's songs were so well thought of in Athens that they were compared with those of Alkman and of Sappho, and were sung at banquets of the nobility.

Of all the poetess-musicians of Greece, the most famous, the one whose very name is almost synonymous with the words "lyric poetry," is Sappho of Lesbos (seventh century B.C.). Lesbos is a triangular island, lying a few miles off the shore of European Turkey— one of those garden islands of the Aegean, full of mountain dells and fresh streams rushing down to the sea, where the small gray olive trees cling to the hillsides, fruit grows sweet and ripe in the valleys, flowers bloom, birds sing, and the sun shines most of the days of the year.

In the seventh century B.C. Lesbos had built up quite a trade with the other Greek islands and the half-Asian, half-Hellenic cities of Asia Minor. And since it was so prosperous, its talented citizens found time and opportunity to bring the art of singing to the lyre to a very high perfection and to take great pains with the music and ceremonial of religious processionals led by women. Here in this tiny island city-state of Lesbos, women had the high social, political, literary, and religious status then common in the Aegean world. They owned their own property and were free to come and go as they pleased. Well educated, especially in poetry and music, they enjoyed the companionship of both men and other women, taking part, as a matter of course, in political and literary discussions. As priestesses in the temples of Lesbos, they served especially Hera, Aphrodite, Demeter, and Artemis. Perhaps no place in all of Greece was more favorable than Lesbos for the flowering of a woman's creative talent, and in this environment Sappho was born, matured, and asserted her leadership.

A woman of independent wealth, highly respected and greatly admired, not only in her own community but throughout Greece, Sappho lived all of her life, with the exception of about five years, in the beautiful surroundings of Lesbos. After her return from her period of political exile in Syracuse she founded a girl's college, or art school as we would call it, to which young women came from far and wide to study poetry and music.

The most gifted of these girls was Erinna. Erinna's mother is said to have chained her to her spinning wheel in order to make her spin rather than sing, or perhaps only to spin while she was singing. But Erinna appears to have found a way to study with Sappho with such

45. The Rāginīs of India represent the ideal graces of womanhood. Bhairaveen, a beautiful maiden, places her flowers on the altar of "Linga" at dawn, when Rāginī Bhairaveen may be sung. This, and other symbolic paintings showing the relation of women to old Indian music, were recently done by Fyzee-Rahamin for his wife, who can sing the six Raga and the thirty Rāginī melodies and who knows the history of their power of enchantment. (See pages 47 and 90.)

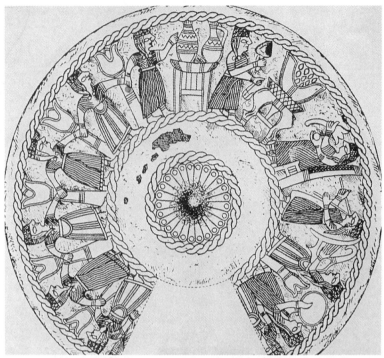

From Perrot-Chipiez. Histoire de l'art dan l'antiquité

46. On a decorated goblet from old Cyprus, the goddess Astarte can be seen with her priestess-musicians. (See page 117.)

Courtesy of Alfred J. Swan

47. A modern Russian painter has portrayed the music of his country as personified by two birdwomen: Sírin and Alkonóst. (See pages 49 and 118.)

48. In Latvia, where women's songs enrich the musical literature, the pagan goddess Laime is represented on a wood-cut receiving a woman's sacrifice. (See page 110.)

49, 50. History is told on pottery. Artemis, accompanied by the dog as symbol of healing power, played magic music but was superseded by Apollo. (See pages 120, 122 and 142.)

success that when she died at nineteen, her poems were already known and admired. It was even said that she could write hexameters better than Sappho. Only one fragment of her work remains, a beautiful lyric song in honor of a dead girl, also a singer—Baucis. Improperly entitled "The Distaff" by later critics, this poem is really a lament, written in hexameter with no refrain but with recurring cries of sorrow.

There appears to have been much affection and pretty displays of endearments among these girls and between them and their slight dark-haired leader and teacher, Sappho. These ways, which are natural enough in any group of girls, later received an unpleasant interpretation among the fourth-century male intelligentsia of Athens, who were openly carrying male homosexuality to a high degree of refined exhibitionism and celebrating it even in works as dignified as the dialogues of Plato. Most modern scholars believe the so-called "Lesbianism" of Sappho and her girls to be only the gossip over wine cups in Athens, where middle-aged literary gentlemen and men about town toasted their own boy flames.

The actual records of Sappho seem to indicate a normal woman's life. She had a little daughter named Cleis. She did some social and poetic sparring with the other most famous poet of Lesbos, a man named Alcaeus. What she and Alcaeus seem to have done is to sing between them a *tenso,* which is a sort of poetical dialogue between kindred spirits. The *tenso* has been an art form from earliest times all over the world, among the Chinese in the pre-Confucian age, among ladies and lords of the medieval court of the Japanese emperor in Kyoto, and among the Tuareg today. The Song of Solomon in the Bible is a *tenso* representing King Solomon's dialogue with Arabian queens whom he courted.

So Alcaeus sang to Sappho: "violet-weaving, pure, sweet smiling Sappho, I wish to say something but shame hinders me."

And Sappho replied, in song: "Hadst thou had desire of aught good or fair, shame would not have touched thine eyes, but thou wouldst have spoken thereof openly." [22]

No one has ever questioned Sappho's genius as a lyric poet. Her fame has lasted for more than twenty centuries. Plato called her the Tenth Muse and Ausonius named her the Muses' Sister. Unfortunately, only a few fragments of the poetry upon which Sappho's fame primarily rests have come down to us; and all of the music with which she accompanied her songs has been lost. But from her own poetry and from relatively contemporaneous accounts in Greek literature, we know her high reputation as a player and singer. She was called "a nightingale of hymns." Her favorite instruments to accompany her songs were the "golden lyre" and the "sweet-toned flute." "Come now, O lyre of mine," she herself sings, "lift up thy voice divine." [23]

Besides accompanying her songs with lyre and flute, Sappho is reputed to have developed for her own use a special kind of stringed instrument called the pectis and to have introduced into musical usage the plectrum, or quill, for striking the lyre's strings. Her creative genius is further illustrated in her invention of new melodies, new forms of music. She is credited with having evolved the mixolydian mode and with having invented a new style of music by breaking up the meter. "This feature," writes one modern admirer, "the Greeks called 'contrast of accent.' In her verse it was like silver things clashing against each other. She buckled together these clashing feet by the golden bands of rhythm and by this means made havoc of emphasis. . . . But when she chose to make symmetry of emphasis, she could. The sapphic meter is a woman's hexameter. It is the feminine heroic." [24]

Sappho and her pupils officiated at public religious festivals as well as at weddings, and Sappho herself may even have been official conductor of the temple choirs. "Come to the splendid temple grounds of Hera of the gleaming eyes, you girls of Lesbos," she writes, "and trip lightly with whirling measure, performing a beautiful choral dance for the goddess; and Sappho shall lead you, her golden lyre in her hand." [25] We have fragments of the beautiful wail laments that Sappho and her girls sang to hasten the rebirth of the child god at festivals to Adonis:

Maidens: Tender Adonis lies adying,
O Cytheria, what were best to do?

Cytheria (Leader): Go, beat your breasts, ye maids, and crying,
Rend ye your robes in sign of rue!" [26]

The subjects of Sappho's lyrics were the subjects important to women, the everyday happenings of their lives. She sang of her love for her little daughter; she wrote love songs and marriage songs; hymns and laments to be sung at religious ceremonies. So famous were her epithalamia or wedding songs that Sappho and her pupils were frequently and widely employed as musicians at weddings. And the poetic form of her epithalamia was the model which other writers used for nearly a thousand years in Greece, Rome, and even Europe. Knowing Sappho's authority in one type of art-song, can we not assume the same for the Egyptian poetess-musicians who created the laments and dirges attributed to the goddess Isis?

In order to judge the quality of Sappho's music, it is unnecessary to have samples of it. Her verses, her melodies, and the strains that accompanied them on flute or lyre were regarded by her contemporaries and by critics of the golden age as bearing the stamp of perfection. Her work had the same quality as the poetry and sculpture of the Periclean Age in Athens. Unquestionably, the music composed by Sappho and her companions, while of course very different from that of our times, was creation of the very highest order by trained musical talent.

Sappho was not a "sport"—a woman gone masculine—as many people have considered her, or an extraordinary deviation from type that might never occur again. She was simply an extremely talented individual, a woman with a great aptitude for poetic-musical expression, who lived in an environment peculiarly favorable for its full development. For her there existed a juxtaposition of the three factors *always* essential to the full unfolding of creative musical imagination. She developed in a culture in which music was an integral part of both informal and formal life. She belonged to a class of people from whom, in that culture, music was expected. As a member of the Aegean society, she inherited melodic impulse. Every artist of the islands had the background of Egypt and Crete for musical assertion in lyric song. Finally, Sappho had training and experience in the technique required by the standards of her community—an outstanding woman, it is true, but intrinsically no different from other exceptionally talented women of her own and of many other communities. What made Sappho the peerless lady of music and song was the fact that she had behind her an immemorial past of experiment by women in poetry and music. Hers was the last perfect flowering of thousands of years of women's song. (See Plate 44.)

CHAPTER VIII

ARTEMIS

1.

FOR creative expression in music there must be a free flow between the plane of daily experience and the plane of thought and fantasy. One must be able to transfer into universal and ideal terms one's vital personal experience. To the extent to which the ideal plane is restricted or distorted, the creative energies of the individual are devitalized or even poisoned.

Women in pre-Christian times all over the world had simply and naturally evolved a grand religious idea out of their greatest experience—the experience of birth. And just as simply and naturally, they assumed that the life of the universe could be expressed in terms of a woman's experience. Surely, they thought, the universal life must be a mother. It might unite with a father. But the motherhood of the deity was to them more obvious and more really important than the fatherhood. They were not restricted, as Western women later were for nineteen hundred years, to a single male god. On the contrary, they had a representation of what they, as women, knew of life. They had a means of idealizing and universalizing their own highest impulses.

Women were pre-eminent in the creation of music in these early times. They are not pre-eminent now. For in those days, they were also pre-eminent in the formulation of religious ideas. They did not take their religion from men, or leave it to men to make their music.

To understand what happened to women later, one must understand the kind of religious images that women had as an inspiration for the outpouring of their songs. In all the myths, rituals, sculpture, painting, and literature of antiquity, there is an all-pervading woman presence. Whether she is called Cybele or Ishtar or Isis or Hera, or some name foreign to our ears, she represents woman power as an active beneficent principle in all life, sometimes as life itself, the ultimate being, mother of all living things. A realized truth generates creative power. From these noble images of women, energy flowed back to the individual woman, releasing and strengthening her imagination and her artistic impulse at this deep level where music is conceived.

Behind the rites of primitive people everywhere today, and in all very early religions, there is the woman spirit. In the great early civilizations of Egypt, Babylonia, and Crete, the Great Mother acquired a grand, all-embracing personality, and was loved and worshiped with a passionate faith. In Rome the cult of the Great Mother persisted and resisted the powerful onslaught of the growing Christian Church until the fifth century. In Greece, where the tendency was to bring all gods down to earth and turn them into human beings, the personality of the Great Mother was split up into a number of divine feminine figures and lovingly individualized, by the Greek talent for character delineation, into ideal women, clearly distinguished from each other in temperament, appearance, and the kind of interest they took in human affairs—but all of them noble, benignant, all-powerful.

The great goddesses, by whatever name they were called, had their own rites, in which music and dancing were always conspicuous, their own liturgies, their own myths, and their own insignia. One had the spiral; others carried the plume, jewels, an ear of corn, the three-stalked flower, a musical instrument. One was crowned with the sun's halo, one held the sky cape above her, another a sea shell. One stood surrounded by the swiftly flowing rivers of the world. Many were accompanied by lions—symbols of the strength inherent in womanhood. All the great goddesses represented the rhythm of life and the moon.

These goddesses, in their many beautiful impersonations, with their various symbols, represent three mighty facts of nature, akin to each other in their character and manifestations, which seemed to these early human beings, and especially to women, to hold the key to life. One was the waxing and waning of the moon, its three nights of darkness, its effulgent period of resplendent light making night for the brief period of the full moon a kind of heavenly day full of mystery and magic. The second was the fact that, in nature, death is the prelude to new birth. When the flower petals fall, there remains the seed from which new flowers will spring. And the third was the kinship of the woman—in all those biological details that distinguish her from the male—to the moon cycle and to the something that gives birth throughout all nature. Hence the divine life was naturally and inevitably feminine and woman was its natural priestess. She knew how to speak to it in her incantations; she knew the rhythms, the gestures, and the symbols, the spirit behind all things that would understand and heed. (See Plate 48.)

2.

As time went on and many, many women worked to perfect their understanding of the ultimate woman power, different goddesses, or different phases of the one great woman spirit, came to represent the woman in her different characters and functions—as mate, mother, worker, musician, and "virgin," or free, unattached to a mate, untrammeled with children.

All the goddesses represented to some degree the woman's life span. But there was one great spirit, the Greek Hera, who represented this the most clearly. She had three distinct forms, corresponding to the three phases of changing life. In the first she was the girl-child, young, fresh, free, having not yet come to maturity. In the second she was a woman of the childbearing age, in the fullness of her peculiar power of womanhood, as mate and mother. In the last she was the woman past childbearing age, but not old, free again, in the ripeness of character, in the profound knowledge of life that motherhood and wifehood nobly fulfilled have brought her.

In the beginning, when Hera first came to Greece from goddess-ruled Crete, she was entirely independent of Zeus. Even in the Olympian age she kept her own temples, priestesses, girl choirs, and rites, in which music and dancing were integrated. Hera was primarily the matron, guardian of marriage, mistress of the home, noble, dignified, and wise. A famous artistic representation of her, of which only a description now remains, showed her seated on a throne, carrying the scepter of world dominion in one hand and in the other a pomegranate—symbol of life.

The concept of mate as distinguished from that of mistress of the home received other impersonations. A dignified god symbolizing mating or sex is rare in the ancient pantheons. The Oriental gods usually represent unbridled male energy. The little boy Cupid or Eros was a frivolous conception of late Greek literature dominated by male intelligentsia, and very trivial and silly in comparison with the mighty, all-powerful goddesses of sex in earlier times, who symbolize the *rhythm* of sex desire.

Of these, one of the oldest was Sumerian Innanna, later Ishtar. In her resided the rhythm of sex desire. When she rested, all procreation ceased. Even the urge for it died until she gave the signal for the rebirth. An ancient myth represented Ishtar descending into hell, or darkness, for three days, corresponding to the three nights of the dark of the moon. On the third day she was revived by two goddesses impersonating the bread of life and the water of life; then, clothed in splendor and beauty, she emerged and roused all living things to mate.

Ishtar was one of the mightiest superhuman powers of all time, known as "Directress of Mankind." She was worshiped in many temples by both women and men. Troops of dancing, singing priestesses and many women officials served her. On the monuments and seals of Sumer she appeared in a long robe with a crown on her head and an eight-pointed star in her hand. From this same Ishtar, beautiful Venus in Rome took her name and her characteristics. In Greece, Ishtar and the idea of deifying sexual love were impersonated by Aphrodite, whose real home was the island of Cyprus. Here, where Cretan culture took early root, Aphrodite was a moon goddess and specifically the bearer of the life-giving dew, or mist, which comes at night. This refreshing moisture was thought to be, like the life-giving seminal fluid, the gift of the moon. Hence Aphrodite was the goddess born of the sea, and also the moon, which influenced, in some obscure magnetic ways, its tides and the sexual rhythm in women. Like other Great Mothers, Aphrodite lamented and made songs of rejoicing over the death and resurrection of her son, Adonis. Everywhere in Greek culture the mighty goddess of the rhythm of life itself and of music was the inspiration of festivals at which the whole populace shared her grief and joy.

In most of these deities of sex there was a recognition of the sex urge as the basis for a higher development of the life of the spirit. But without woman's authority in regulating the rhythm of sex life, spiritual life also lay dormant. As if to symbolize woman's life-giving power in affairs of the spirit, one of the old Oriental goddesses was depicted holding the material substance of the world encased in a spiritual essence. This image may be regarded as representing the meaning of all ancient feminine deities—unity of the higher human faculties with the natural and real things of the earth.

3.

Nearly all great goddesses were mothers and often passed on the torch of life to the next generation by their own power. Many of them had names whose roots indicated their function. The last part of the Greek Demeter's name means mother. A present day South Indian word for "nurse" or "mother" is "amma," and it is incorporated into the Great Mothers' names, such as Nukalamma. In representations of the mother goddess, her maternal functions were universalized by associating various symbols of life and the rhythm of life with the figure of the woman. In picture after picture the Great Mother sits on her throne holding, not a child, but the more comprehensive emblem of the phial containing the water of life. She beats a drum, not only because real women use a drum as a magic device to assist childbirth, but because her life is bound to rhythm. She sings, not only because real mothers sing to their children, giving them their first impressions of melody, but because the music of the spheres resounds to human ears only through the door of life she opens for both body and soul.

With only local variations in the different countries, the Great Mother was the focus of celebrations for changes in the seasons and for the reappearance of the new moon.

The goddess gave a child to the world, fashioned out of her own body and blood. She gave nourishment that her child might thrive— first her own milk and then cultivated foods. The child was sometimes a son and sometimes a daughter. Demeter gave Kore, a beautiful clean-limbed, clear-eyed maiden. Other goddesses had both a maiden and a youth. Cybele's child, Attis, was double-sexed. The offspring of the Great Mother was often identified with the fruits of the earth and became the symbol of regeneration, to be lamented and rejoiced over by the goddesses and their semidivine attendants. Every year or so, at great national festivals, Ishtar mourned for Tammuz, Isis for Osiris, Cybele for Attis, Aphrodite for Adonis, and Demeter for Kore. Rites for the rebirth were the most important rites and they were ceremonies of the goddess-mother, not the godfather. It was the mother's sacrifice, the mother's power for bringing life, the mother's point of view that gave the religion of those times its character and appeal.

As mother, the goddess created the world in co-operation with a male deity, to whom, with a grim feminine realism, the early priest-ess-theologians assigned the lesser part in this mighty achievement. It would have been impossible, in those honest early days, to convince a woman who had borne children that the father's part in projecting life was the greater part and should be so represented in the creation of divine images. Running through all the early stories of the creation there is also the idea that a male god can never do much until a woman puts real life into him or his work. Prometheus once made a youth, but it was Athene who pressed the spiritual substance into his brain. The shepherd boy Endymion led a passive existence on Mount Latmos until Selene, the Full-Moon Mother, embraced him. Inspired by her magic touch, he began to dream of noble thoughts and deeds. Again, in one of the Nile legends the river is a male spirit that flows between two banks represented by a goddess. She stands with outstretched arms, as though begging for the water to come and fertilize her. But the mighty river swelled and flowed only when Isis let fall her tears of mourning for Osiris, the Nile god. The goddess had to make the wailing and the weeping that always brings about the rebirth.

In a hymn of remarkable vigor, Indrānī, one of the Seven Mothers in India, chanted the dogma of her superiority over her husband: "I am the banner and the head, a mighty arbitress am I! I am victorious and my Lord shall be submissive to my will. I am victorious o'er my Lord, my song of triumph is supreme." [1]

The women theologians did not generally assume that even a goddess could create the world without a mate. The oldest company of Egyptian deities consisted of four pairs of consorts with equal powers. Throughout Egyptian history most of the well-known gods had their female counterparts functioning in exactly the same way. The old Babylonian creation myth told of the primeval ocean flood containing male and female elements. Oriental gods still have their *śakti*—their female half without whom they would be powerless.

As mother, the goddess could compel rebirth. Rites for the rebirth were the most important features of early cults, and in them emphasis was placed on women's attitudes rather than on men's. Ishtar rejuvenated her son Tammuz by holding him on her knees. Demeter displayed an ear of corn as the symbol of power to bring about rebirth. The woman's power of self-sacrifice for the sake of others, the mother's authority in regeneration is beautifully expressed in the story of the rebirth of Osiris. This popular Egyptian god, who personified the life-giving river Nile, was murdered by Set, the Typhoon, and cut into fourteen pieces as a symbol of the waning moon, which takes that number of nights to disappear from the sky. His mate, Isis, Creatrix of Green Things, determined to save his life. Alone and exhausted almost to the point of death, she persevered until she had found the scattered pieces of his body. Nūt, the Sky Mother, united and regenerated the dead god. "She gives to thee thy head and thy legs, she joins the limbs together, and replaces thy heart in thy body." [2] Then Isis conceived by Osiris and bore the child Horus. Without her persistence in the face of dire distress and her overpowering love, life on earth might have remained dormant—symbolically speaking—forever.

Of all the goddess-mothers, Isis was the greatest, just as Ishtar was the greatest of all goddesses of sex. In her the idea of mother love was sublimated into an altruistic, civilizing force capable of leading men and women to a higher level of intelligent living. Springing from other earlier mother-spirits of the preliterate age, she was more widely worshiped in Egypt by both women and men than any other goddess there. She survived until the sixth century A.D., spreading her influence in Greece and Rome. An old Greek inscription shows the reverence accorded her in magnificent terms:

I am Isis, mistress of every land; I laid down laws for mankind and ordained things that no one may change; I am she who governs Sirius the Dog-Star; I am she who is called divine among women; I divided the earth from the heaven; I made manifest the paths of the stars; I prescribed the course of the sun and the moon; I found out the labours of the sea; I made justice mighty. I burdened woman with the newborn babe in the tenth month; I ordained that parents should be believed by their children; I put an end to cannibalism; I overthrew the sovereignty of tyrants; I compelled women to be believed by men; I made justice more mighty than gold or silver; I made virtue and vice to be distinguished by instinct. [3]

4.

The woman as mate evolves into the woman as mother. The woman as mother is a worker for her family, and as such she evolves into the presiding spirit of community work and welfare. There were many women spirits in all parts of the ancient world who reflected women's work and activities as extensions of the functions of motherhood. There was Ishtar, the potter; Nëit, the weaver; the spinning and singing Fates; Athene, worker in the art and crafts of civilized life. Innanna, the great Sumerian mother and goddess came to the aid of women in childbirth with the words: "Maiden of the place of begetting am I; in the home where the mother gives birth, a protecting shadow am I!" [4] Many goddesses had the power of healing and carried the magic wand entwined with serpents later held by Aesculapius. Egyptian Taweret, called The Great One, presided over family affairs and symbolized ancient woman's authority in the home—the focal point for bringing life and for making music.

The most remarkable example of the way the ancients were thinking out the relation between private home and community was to be found in the impersonation and functions of the goddess Hestia in Greece and of Vesta in Rome. Since primitive women today are generally the keepers of a perpetual fire, these goddesses probably symbolized a very old association of woman with authority over the hearth. Hestia and Vesta were the guardians of the hearth in its twofold aspect, as symbol of the internal unity of the family and of hospitality to the stranger. As impersonations of hospitality, they were hostesses of suppliants and fugitives who might invoke the sacredness of the family hearth where they had taken refuge and so be protected. Hestia's home was in the prytaneum, where a fire, representing the common hearth for the whole city, was kept ever going. Colonists traveling from the city to settle elsewhere received a coal from the fire, as symbol of the continuity of life in their new home with that in their old. Similarly the Roman Vesta, a very ancient goddess, became an important state deity whose vestal virgins guarded the sacred fire and the Sybilline books with their treasured secrets of the way to live.

The Greeks expressed their sense of the communal importance of woman's work and authority by adopting a specific goddess as the guardian of a city. Of these personifications of woman as worker and manager, the most complete and authoritative is that of Athene, guardian of Athens. In this noble figure was concentrated the highest qualities of the feminine personality as shown in work and public leadership. She was the goddess of the pure ether, the dawn and the twilight, and goddess, in her moments of righteous wrath, of the thunder cloud and the lightening bolt. She was the guardian of women's arts and industries, protector of family and community life. As guardian of peaceful industry, Athene was goddess of peace. But to ensure peace she would go to war, resolutely and thoughtfully. In war she was goddess of counsel and prudent strategy as opposed to her reckless brother Ares, who represented brute courage and violence. The heroes like Odysseus whom she led and protected were "wise." They used their heads. They exercised forethought, they strove to overcome brawn and violence with intelligence and management.

In the many statues of Athene power and benign authority seem to be guiding the hand of the artist in the molding of the noblest kind of feminine face, with its broad, open brow, candid, thoughtful eyes (which in the Greek statues were carefully painted in), and firm, kind, resolute mouth. She stands with helmet on her head, shield and lance in her hand, the leader of states, the supreme authority in civilized life, the sure, unruffled, unflinching guardian of all that is under her care.

Such authority as Athene wielded might even be conceived of as extending beyond private hearth and city hearth to the whole world and to the universe itself. As a mother weaves her children's clothes, Nëit in Egypt wove the warp and woof of the world's fabric. The Fates (the Teutonic Norns) occupied their time in spinning. The threads they span and cut were the threads not of garments, but of life.

5.

As mate, mother, provider for the household through industry, and guardian of home and community hearths, the woman sang at the altar to invoke the universal life for the protection of lives under her care. So she was, by necessity of her motherhood, a musician. In every country of the ancient world, divine symbols represented women in their role as dancers, instrumental players, and especially as singers.

The dance had many feminine and few masculine impersonations. All nymphs, fairies, and forest mothers danced. In India the Apsaras were in perpetual motion. In Greece the Horae danced to mark the march of time. The Charites, the Horae, and the Graces—symbols of the bloom of youth—moved with measured steps under their own leader, Thalia. The Greeks portrayed religious dance as a matron.

In Crete the great Mother Rhea "invented" the steps that made the Cretan youth famous for centuries. In Egypt, Hat-hor was goddess of the moon and goddess of the dance.

Musical instruments were often the property of spirits and goddesses. A certain type of drum was sacred only to Sarasvati, giver of speech and music to humanity, but various types of drums, tambourines, and cymbals belonged to the company of deified musicians. The Bacchae always carried them, and Cybele, the All-Begetting Mother, beat a drum to mark the rhythm of life. Flutes were also played by the Bacchae and by many others. A legend tells that Athene invented the instrument that blew the breath of life. To Isis was attributed the invention of the sistrum, a glorified type of rattle. Lyres and harps of different types were associated with supernatural musicians, especially Artemis. In Persia the spirit of the harp was personified by Azada, whose music echoed the harmony of the spheres. (See Plate 46.)

Singing was the genius of goddesses. Each separate step in the making of magic song became deified. The wail, the cry of joy, the imitation of natural sounds all had feminine impersonation. Every type of song—incantation, epic, lament—had a special feminine spirit.

As a result of its constant use upon occasions of birth and rebirth, the wail received impersonation. Little figures of clay or marble, representing women as wailers and weepers, have been found in the graves and on the sarcophagi of many peoples. When her son Ruadan was born, the Celtic goddess Anu gave the first wail ever heard in Ireland. Ishtar wailed "like a woman in travail" in her effort to bring about the return of creative energy to the sleeping earth. Isis invented the wail and taught it to the women of her country as a magical device to bring about birth. The Great Wailer herself, accompanied by Nephthys, her sister, the Less Wailer; Neget, a goddess known as the crier; Nëit and Nūt, two of the Great Mothers; Selket, protectress of the dead; and two lesser deities, Ibwet and Tayet, stood in the temple of Hat-hor at Denderah in the room consecrated to lamentations, ready to wail the image of Osiris back to life.

Wail songs, or laments, were composed by many supernatural women. All nymphs, forest mothers, and other semidivine creatures sang laments. The sirens, as playmates of Persephone, goddess of death, personified death lamentations—incantations to bring about rebirth. But whenever sirens appeared upon tombstones, they were depicted as both lamenting and rejoicing. In the earliest times they assumed the form of bird-women, and as such may be relatives of Sírin and Alkonóst, the two Russian bird-women from whom came all laments and songs of joy. (See Plate 47.)

A link between fantastical bird-women and real women singers is the common myth of women turning into birds. In Greece there were two such legends. In one, Aedon killed her son by mistake and prayed to be turned into a bird. "Daughter of Pandareus, the brown bright nightingale," wrote the poet, "pours forth her full-voiced music, bewailing her child." [5] In the other myth, two sisters are turned into birds and bemoan their sorrows. Philomela became a swallow and Procne a nightingale. (Ovid twisted the names—probably on purpose, as Philomela is the prettier sound.) Both bird-sisters lament. Pausanias, always interested in the origin of myths, explained: "The tradition of the change into the nightingale and swallow is, I think, because these birds have a melancholy song like a lament." [6] The significance of Pausanias' interpretation is that neither he nor anyone else, apparently, thought it odd for a woman to be identified with a songbird when in reality only male birds sing.

The same association is found in Lithuania, where the verb "to cuckoo" signifies "to lament" and where the cuckoo is nearly always compared to a woman. The reason this identification did not seem incongruous is undoubtedly because the association of women with the singing of laments was so strong that the sex of the bird dwindled into unimportance. All mother-goddesses, too, sang the laments and the songs of rejoicing. In Egypt, Isis and her sister Nephthys composed the laments that became the models for both informal and formal dirges. In other countries the name of the mother is mentioned in the lament as the one who is mourning and rejoicing.

Other types of incantations—those for achieving any purpose—often assumed human guise. The singing Sirens, for example, could influence the behavior of people, animals, and even natural phenomena. They could inspire some men to great and noble deeds; they could lure others from their chosen pursuits and chain them fast. Only the Great Mothers surpassed them in the art of making incantations. Nearly every one had a subtitle such as "Lady of Incantations."

In the mythology of ancient Rome, the Carmentes were pesonifications of the fortune or luck of the mother in childbirth, but they were also projections of the incantations made by midwives, whose chief means of assistance at childbirth was music. The Carmentes got their name from the word *carmen*, meaning a charm, and incantation or song. *Carmen* is derived from the name of a real person, Carmenta or Nicostrata, an ancient poetess of Latium, who is said to have introduced religion, poetry, and agriculture. She seems to have been a prophetess, bard, and cult heroine. To us the translation of *carmen* is more familiar as "song" than as "magic formula for aid in childbirth." The shift from the original specific meaning to the more generic one must have resulted from the innumerable incantations or songs made through the ages by women for aid in childbirth.

Not only each separate department of music had a special goddess, but the art itself was generally given a feminine impersonation. As we have already seen, some of the very ancient goddesses combined music with their other life-giving functions. Hat-hor, Bastet, Sarasvati, Bhāratī, Innanna, Artemis, and the Muses were all identified with singing and dancing and the playing of certain instruments.

The Muses, at first only three in number, had names that indicated their business. One was called Invention, or She Who Invents the Words and Musical Phrases. Another was known simply as Song, or The One Who Sings. The third Muse answered to Memory, or She Who Remembers, an important quality in an age when song and story were passed orally from singer to singer. This one inherited her name, her faculty, and her function from her mother, Mnemosyne. One very old set of their names was Nete, Mese, and Hypate. These also signify the low, middle, and high tones in the Greek system of scales. Such designations would not have been associated with feminine spirits if an identity with music had not been intended. In the oldest depictions of the Muses, they stand with a woman leader, sometimes Mnemosyne, sometimes Athene, sometimes an unknown figure—possibly Artemis. Throughout their long history the Muses, from whose very name the word music is derived, kept their musical authority. Around Zeus's altar they alone chanted the epic of the world's origin. Thamyris, the bard, was struck blind for daring to challenge them in song. Even after Apollo had acquired the title "God of Music," he rarely dared appear without their encircling support.

Taking the music deities from many ancient countries as a whole, we can thus reconstruct a complete hierarchy of women whose prestige and authority survives to the present day in painting and in literature. Chief among them were the Great Mothers. They were surrounded by specialized deities of lesser rank. Then came groups like the Bacchae—the mothers who brought Dionysos to birth— various grades of Forest Mothers, Heroines, Nymphs, Seasons, Hours, Nereids, Graces, Apsaras, Gift-bringers of Plenty such as the Char- ites, Fates, Sirens, other bird-women, even witches. These creatures were eternally dancing, playing instruments, and singing. When male spirits are found in their ranks, they come as consorts. The Gandharvas, a group of Indian spirits, were husbands of the beauti- ful dancing Apsaras.

When and where the first of these spirits of women's music was projected is a mystery. Many of them appear as fully developed and powerful musicians in the earliest strata of literature. In India, there were Sarasvati and Bhāratī; in Egypt, Bastet and Hat-hor; in Sumer, Innanna. In Greece, the Muses belong to the oldest company—Ar- temis, too, has been traced to the most ancient times. With various attributes, she was widely worshiped long before her so-called brother Apollo entered the scene and usurped her authority in music. (See Plate 49.)

In the beginning, these oldest goddesses undoubtedly reflected the musical activities of real women. In later times, when primitive naïveté gave way to sophistication and to what is called learning, they often became glorified into abstractions. The Muses, their num- ber augmented to three times three, came to represent wisdom and knowledge. Terpsichore, She who Loves to Dance, became the ab- stract choral dance. Calliope, the One who Loves to Sing, became abstract epic poetry; Euterpe became lyric poetry; Melpomene, tragedy; Erate, erotic poetry; Klio, the storyteller became history; and Urania, from She who Dwells in the Heavens, meaning the moon and the stars, became astronomy. From images of the waxing, full, and waning moon, Artemis, with Selene, Hekate, and the dancing nymphs became the symbols of harmony and order in the universe. Anahita, Aphrodite, and Venus, from being personifications of sexual love became symbols of life—and symbols of music.

From the historical point of view, the music goddesses as abstrac- tions, although very grand and noble figures, have tended to obscure rather than to fortify the former association of women with music. It requires a mental effort to accept an image such as Urania, muse of astronomy. In our culture, women astronomers are too rare to warrant their idealization. But Urania as She who Dwells in the Heavens is readily comprehensible to anyone. It is less difficult to accept the Great Mother, creatrix and ruler, because in everyone's experience, there is somewhere a mother giving birth and managing a baby. But if we can recognize a real woman in a divine Mother, why can we not recognize a real musician in a divine Music-Maker? Only because, in our culture, women have not so distinguished themselves. Without being oversublimated, Calliope, the One who Loves to Sing, and Klio, the One who Tells Stories, are obvious enough as reflections of reality. To them and others of their kind we must turn for an understanding of the woman-musician's past. Divested of vague and visionary attributes, the goddess-musicians are historical evidence, revealing real musicians of high creative intelligence and power.

6.

A woman, by reason of her sex, is mate and mother, and in performing her functions as such evolves naturally into worker, community manager, and musician. But even so, she must remain a human soul, free, unenthralled to sex, an individual self, which is a single expression of humanity. This idea of the freedom of the self in womanhood was very precious to women of ancient times, overburdened, as they tended to be, by work and maternity. The determination to keep some freedom is expressed in the secret societies, among women everywhere, for whose rites women escape from children and household to the hills.

The supreme example among goddesses of this ideal of free selfhood is Artemis. She represents at once the creative individual who meets life with a proud, positive attitude and the creative freedom of collective womanhood. Artemis, the Maid, had no mate; she was not a mother, and remained forever "virgin," that is, herself, reflecting the value placed by the ancients on womanhood as an independent spiritual power. Coming from societies in which women predominated in religious and musical life, and in which men musicians admitted their debt to women by wearing feminine costumes, Artemis carried the lyre, an old moon-cult female symbol. Until late in Greek history, Artemis Hegemonia (leader) or Artemis Hymnia accompanied the lyre-playing Apollo, who dressed and wore his hair like his mother, Leto, or his great sister. (See Plate 50.)

Artemis as the protector of all young things and guardian of wild life was the protector also of women against the too insistent demands of Aphrodite—of sex and childbearing. She was woman, free, fleet of foot, strong of limb, serene of soul, woman as a creature of nature, forever untamed, able to slip out of the grasp of any man and take herself on her swift feet to the hills. Nothing could bind her. In many Greek representations of her she stands with her robe girt up and her hair bound for swift movement, with a hind, symbol of all fleet-footed wild life, at her side, and bow and arrows in her hand, ready to shoot a dart at anyone who would stop her.

Today Artemis is often misrepresented as the goddess of chastity —a sterile title indeed for the great moon spirit. When Sappho sang about herself, "I am forever virgin," [7] she knew that Artemis was integrity, the self; the part of the individual soul that must preserve its independence or perish. And as such she received the sacrifices of many women of Sappho's age. Among the most inspiring of these votive offerings is the small ivory figurine of the triple moon goddess holding the torch of life for the lovely dancing Daughters of the Moon. (See frontispiece.)

7.

Mate, mother, worker, communal guardian, musician, and free soul—such was woman's picture of herself in the thousands of years in which she worked out her own idealizations of her own functions and sang freely at altars of her own building to the great goddesses and their hosts of spirit attendants. Mirrors of woman in her different natures, avatars of the strength that can alter—as the moon alters— and yet preserve the feminine core,[8] they also symbolized life in its many manifestations. What the natural woman was, what she did, became the highest object of religious devotion, and so idealized and universalized, became an ever revered inspiration to effort and invention.

Before these spirits, the holy hymn of an ancient faith was chanted. Worshiping nature's rhythmic laws and striving to keep in touch with the life force, which is beyond human comprehension, men and women set a spiritual value on woman's natural way. Men and women both lived according to the principle that woman is creative in body and spirit. In the independence and originality of the spirit of collective womanhood, which was and remains the glory of primitive religion, a woman may have faith and courage —and the heart—to sing. When Artemis strikes her lyre, she sings no man's composition, and lifts her eyes to no man's heaven. She sings for herself, out of the deepest truths she knows as a woman, in the reassuring and lovely splendor of the moon at its full.

THE DARK OF THE MOON

CHAPTER IX

THE TWILIGHT OF THE GODDESS

1.

ABOUT 500 B.C. there fell on these hopeful civilizations of our earth a kind of creeping blight. It did not come all at once, but slowly in a change here and a change there that may have seemed at first a great improvement in the organization of life or a correction of a local abuse. Indeed, the Chinese, who went further than any other people in carrying out the new ideas, say flatly that real civilization began at the moment when men determined to know who their own children were and to assume responsibility for their care and education. This was, indeed, a change for the better—or might have been for the better if more intelligence had been shown in carrying it out.

But the men, in taking over, did it crudely. Their idea of making sure that their children were their own was to shut the women up from the moment they could bear a child, out of sight and hearing and contact with any man but a predestined father. In China they achieved this in the end by so crippling the women that they could not move beyond their own homes and courtyards unless they were carried. The long slow process of foot-binding began in childhood and continued through years and years of torture. At puberty, shame and fear descended on the girl, for now she was really a menace to society. She must be watched with all eyes and barred with all bars.

How different from the customs of the mothers, even among very primitive tribes, with their incantations to the moon, their holy baths, torch races, songs, dances, and flowers! Primitive mothers sometimes put the girls through very trying ordeals. But behind these ordeals is the grand sense of destiny, the taking up of the women's burden with pride and congratulation, the initiation into the sense of oneness with all birth and being.

The new attitudes were formulated in the hard, clean-cut maxims of Confucius, which became the official religion of China and the foundation of its education. Confucius was a wise man. But he was also the world's worst prude. He thought it immoral for a man's coat and a woman's dress to hang side by side on pegs on a wall. No wonder that Mme Sun Yat-sen, the great wife of the great leader of modern China, says that if China is to live, Confucianism must go. Yet even in China there are indications of an earlier and better day, astonishing to one who knows the pruderies of Chinese life even now wherever it is not yet touched by the spirit of such women as Mme Sun Yat-sen.

What life in China was like just before Confucius became its law-giver one may guess from the lays of Che-king, which Confucius edited. These lays represent the ancient customs of country people. As among primitive people today, the men and women were like two separate tribes and had each their own functions and collective activities. The men were farmers, the women weavers, having learned the art of raising silk worms from the wife of Huang-ti. This separation is indicated in a Chinese legend in which two stellar deities represent the female weaver and the male ox driver. Between them spreads the milky way, the Celestial River.

But according to the legend, this Celestial River could be crossed once a year. So, also, the peasant girls and boys had a spring festival to relieve the hard, monotonous toil of daily life and to awaken in them the joy of living. In the province of Honan they used to have a celebration that was very different from anything allowed well-brought-up Chinese girls after Confucius reformed China for the benefit of men.

This great seasonal celebration was the time for social intercourse and the sanctioned hour for the young people to meet and mate. At the spring rites the girls first bathed in the life-giving river, then exchanged flowers with the boys and played games that suggested the flight of birds as they pursue each other seeking a mate. The boys and the girls challenged each other in song, the girls drawing from their own experience as they gave the invitation. Since they were accustomed to weave both plain and flowered material, they sang:

"In a flowered skirt, in a plain skirt—
In a flowered robe, in a plain robe—

"Come, sirs! Come sirs!
Take me in the chariot to your home!" [1]

The boys prepared their own mind for courtship by suggesting that spring was in the air:

"Withered leaves, withered leaves,
The wind comes to blow upon you."

The girls expressed their longing:

"Until I have seen my lord—
My restless heart, ah, how it beats—
But as soon as I am united to him,
Then my heart will be at peace." [2]

The two groups danced and sang in antiphonal choruses, each group having its own leader and each group bringing to the festival its own musical contribution.

In this primitive festival, the origin of the symbolic sacred marriage of so many ancient societies is suggested. What was at first in the childhood of humanity a natural way to sanction sex intercourse became dignified in many ancient societies into a formal religious ceremony performed as a symbolic act by kings and queens to bring health and wealth to their people.

2.

While China was thus "civilizing" itself, by repressing women's rites and music, a great change had already come over India. As we have seen, the early Aryan people there had worshiped a trinity of great goddesses—Sarasvati, Bhāratī, and Ilā—who symbolized women's participation in both the religious rite and in music. At first the Aryan conquerors had held women in high esteem, and women had performed the sacrifices at the altars and had sung their hymns. It may be that the tendency to lock women up was intensified by the rabid color prejudices of the Aryans, who were determined not to mingle their blood with the darker native race, a prejudice that also created the great evils of the caste system. However this may be, Indian women fell under the blight of a peculiarly fanatical male fear of their sex.

Even before the spirit of Confucius froze down upon the early naturalness and joy of China, an old pedant named Manu in India had decided to put the singing women in their place and let man take over and perform the sacrifices, including those that women had invented out of their own intimate and unique faith as child-bearers and life bearers. Manu's regulations said, among other things: "No act is to be done according to her own will by a young girl, a young woman, or even by an old woman, though in their own houses. In her childhood, a girl should be under the will her father; in her youth, of her husband; her husband being dead, of her sons; a woman should never enjoy her own will. . . . Though of bad conduct or debauched, or even devoid of good qualities, a husband must always be worshiped like a god by a good wife." [3] This attempt to silence women was followed by a resolve to curse her very nature. Manu insisted upon woman's intrinsic wickedness. She was spiritu-ally inferior to man—identified with the Sudra, the lowest order of life, akin to brute beasts. She must not participate in religious cere-monies, she must not study the sacred books, she must not even hear them read. Manu announced: "No religious ceremony for women should be accompanied by mantras (except marriage)—with these words the rule of right is fixed; for women being weak creatures and having no share in the mantras, are falsehood itself. So stands the law." [4]

Among the Brahmans, then, women ceased to function as a be-neficent power. Although some of the goddesses survived in Hindu theology, woman as a living creature became associated with in-significance and even with evil. She existed merely to serve her husband and to bear the son who alone could open for the father the door of eternal life. Her marriage meant not a fulfillment of her individuality, but a sacrifice of herself even to the point of ending her own life when her lord died. This absorption of her personality into another's was reflected in a famous epic sung by women while grinding corn at the hand mill. Innumerable verses describe how Basti Singh's wife was wooed by a dishonorable brother-in-law who had murdered her husband; how the wife pretended to submit in order to ensure a proper burial for her husband; how, when she saw his corpse, her purity ignited the funeral pyre and burned not only the dead body but herself as well.

Manu's law for women resulted in the erection of a barrier between women and music entirely different from the taboos existing in the primitive tribes. There the barriers consist of local taboos upon special activities and almost never a denial of ability. Manu's barrier was different, too, from the limitations placed upon women by the Egyptians. In Egypt, woman and her goddess were always regarded as a dynamic and a beneficent influence, indispensable to the common weal. But the Brahmans established a theory that woman was not merely insignificant in the scheme of life but was actually a malignant force. Here was the sinister threat to self-reverence, to dignity, and to integrity of spirit. Here was a body blow to the principle that feminine urges are a dynamic power for advancing civilization. This took away from women the expectation that they would collectively develop their confidence in their powers and in their importance as a beneficent influence on humanity, backed by a sincere and universal respect by men for them as such. No one with such a handicap can become a creative musician.

3.

The threat to women musicians gathered tremendous momentum in the religious ideas of the Jews. Their history, as it concerns the relation of women to the life of the spirit, is strikingly similar to that of the Brahmans.

The Jews of the Biblical age had inherited some of their beliefs from the ancient Sumerians, who were worshipers of moon deities and especially of Ishtar and her son Tammuz. Other ideas and customs came to the Jews from the Hittites, also a goddess-worshiping people who identified Ishtar with the sun. Still other traditions came from the nomad tribes who wandered with their flocks and herds around the Arabian desert, slowly drifting into Palestine. In the very early days of this migration—about 3000 B.C.—the god of the Hebrews was Yahveh. Like so many other deities of that period, Yahveh was man-woman together. In some tribes he was male with a wife called Anat.

The women of these tribes displayed a strength that corresponded to the woman power represented in the male-female deity. In the oldest part of the Bible, women appear as chieftains, judges, and magicians. Deborah was a prophetess and a judge in Israel. She also possessed magic powers, as Barak well knew. When Deborah commanded the warrior to go against Sisera, the Canaanite, Barak refused to go unless she went with him and lent him the authority of her presence. The oldest existing fragment of Hebrew literature tells of the murder of the enemy of Jael and finally of Deborah's song of triumph.

> "Hear, O ye kings; give ear, O ye princes;
> I, even I, will sing unto the Lord:
> I will sing praise to the Lord God of Israel." [5]

Although the whole hymn is clearly Deborah's, there are some verses that seem to have been chanted antiphonally. Possibly Deborah led her rejoicing women and Barak led his warriors:

> "Awake, awake, Deborah, awake, awake, utter a song!"

To which the reply is:

> "Arise, Barak, and lead thy captivity captive."

And one chorus sang:

> "At her feet he bowed, he fell, he lay down."

Answered by the other:

> "Where he bowed, there he fell down dead." [6]

The chorus was a medium through which the patriotism of the entire tribe could flow. As long as the Jews continued to be a nation of warriors, women were expected to rejoice over victories collectively with their own leaders. When Moses and Aaron led the Hebrews out of Egypt and when the hosts of Pharaoh were drowned in the Red Sea, their sister Miriam, as prophetess and leader of the women, "took a timbrel in her hand; and all the women went out after her with timbrels and with dances." [7] And Miriam sang in triumph antiphonal response to the chorus of Moses and his men. "Sing ye to the Lord, for he hath triumphed gloriously; the horse and his rider hath he thrown into the sea." [8]

Years after Miriam we find Judith, with courage and craft, seducing and slaying Holofernes, captain of the invading Assyrians. On her return, and after the defeat of the enemy, all the women of Israel, in gratitude and thanksgiving, ran together to see Judith "and bless her, and made a dance among them for her . . . and she went before all the people in the dance, leading all the women: and all the men of Israel followed in their armour with garlands, and with songs in their mouths. . . . Then Judith began to sing this thanksgiving in all Israel, and all the people sang after her this song of praise. And Judith said, Begin unto my God with timbrels, sing unto my Lord with cymbals: tune unto him a new psalm: exalt him and call upon his name." [9]

Women's and girls' choruses are mentioned all through the Old Testament. Girl choirs, organized for the antiphonal singing of Psalms—such as Psalm 9—performed at public festivals. In this connection, the three daughters of a certain Levite priest are mentioned as being excellent musicians. Under King Solomon, an enthusiastic lover of music, the girl choirs performed in his second temple and also in his court orchestra. "I gat me men singers and women singers, and the delights of the sons of men as musical instruments, and that of all sorts." [10]

Like all other women of ancient times, Jewish women participated, as a matter of course, in religious ceremonies and in formal secular music. They also carried on their ancient rituals common to women the world over. Wailing to bring the rebirth was expected of them. The prophet Jeremiah called for the mourning women that they might come with their cunning and their knowledge. Sometimes to make their wailing more effective, they sat on drums—symbols of the rhythm of life. Dancing and singing, these natural musicians were creating, as they still are today, beautiful songs for christenings and weddings, for work and for play.

But as it was with the Brahmans, so with the Jews. Men's superior physical strength, necessarily emphasized and developed for aggressive warfare, began to dominate in the life of the spirit. Women gradually lost their prestige and authority. As the years passed, barriers between women and the affirmation of womanhood became firmly established. The ark—always like a ship, a symbol of the womb—remained the holy of holies for the Israelites, but it was guarded by men only. Women, excluded from the priesthood, were forbidden to enter the inner temple. The girl choirs did not sing in the most sacred place. Eventually, women became associated with spiritual inferiority and even with a definitely evil influence. In men's invention of the story of creation, the female was represented as having done humanity a gross disservice. Theologians could not deny that Eve possessed the secret of life and that Adam learned it only by receiving the apple (or pomegranate)—symbol of life and knowledge—from her. But they satisfied their craving for superiority by ordaining that Eve, instead of being reverenced for her power, should be humiliated for her audacity. Jewish men, to this day, thank God in public prayer that they are not born women.

No feminine attributes were mirrored in Jehovah, the fierce warrior God, who guaranteed never to change the rhythm of life. The numerous passages in the Bible alluding to Jehovah's unchanging character refer to the difference between him and the mother-goddesses of the moon cults, whose energy waxed and waned like that of the moon. The ancient practice of lamenting yearly for Tammuz, son of Ishtar, was branded as heresy. No wailing, no rejoicing with the Great Mother was to be tolerated. Much of Old Testament history deals with the struggles of the grim followers of the male warrior god Yahweh to keep their people from straying off to the more attractive altars of the kindlier feminine deities. There is no god but Yahweh, they said. All other idealizations of life, all personifications of the life force, were to be barred. If one could not lift one's soul in faith and adoration to this harsh, unforgiving, unchanging male, the soul must die. "For I the Lord thy God am a jealous God"—so spoke God to man and man to woman.

When women's rites did survive in formal religious ceremonies, men directed them. A good example is the rite of reintegration into normal life after the great experience of childbirth. Instead of being celebrated by women alone, as it always was among primitive people, it passed into the hands of men. The mother required "purification" by a priest.

Exclusion from the intellectual life of their times, exclusion from the spiritual life of men, identification with the unwanted, the undesirable, and the inferior, all contributed to the establishment of a diametrically opposed relation of men to music and of women to music.

Men had, in the male god, a symbol of their own sex; they had officials to perform their rites. They had, furthermore, the sanction of the group to regard their own activities, rites, and modes of expression as the proper expression for all the community. Women's divine images were banished with fire and sword, and women's rites revised or distorted into worship of the male god as the only God.

So Jewish men became the group expected to create the national literature and music. Jewish women did not lose their inherent power to express emotions in the language of music; but they were gradually excluded from the group preferred to make the important music of their times. Women's songs of joy and songs of sorrow ceased to have value for the religious leaders, ceased to be inscribed in the national annals. These leaders even said that for a woman to be seen with her hair uncovered was a disgrace, for a woman to sing verged on unchastity, and that the very hearing of a woman's voice was indecent.

Beginning with Ezekiel (26:113), the prophets warned women: "And I will cause the noise of thy songs to cease; and the sound of thy harps shall be no more heard." [11] And for many centuries the rabbis held to this murderous attitude. "Music in a house must bring that house to destruction." [12] As a consequence of such ideas, the artist singer did not perform solo songs in public from about 300 B.C. until long after 100 A.D., nor did the association of the natural strength and beauty of women's voices with seduction and lust lose force for many more centuries.

The fact that Jewish women had reached this low estate at the time of the birth of Christian culture has a direct bearing upon the relation of women to the music of our times. St. Paul, the first great doctrinaire of the early Christians, saw through Jewish eyes the immediate solution to many of the social problems of his times. It was largely Paul who took the lead in transmitting the prejudices of the ancient Jews toward women to the Christian world then in the making.

4.

In Greece the revolution was slow. Up until about 200 B.C. some women were attending the old colleges for priestesses and some were even organizing new colleges for the study of philosophy and music. Nevertheless, by about 400 B.C. Greek women were feeling the strong impact of male aggression in the institution of the state. School, church, art center, amusement place, and forum became integrated under one control, wholly masculine. Men cultivated a sex solidarity and favored men teachers, men religious officials, men artists, men dramatists and actors.

As a part of this usurpation of authority, men attempted to take over the art of healing, which like magic and music had always been, and is still subconsciously, regarded as an evidence of supernatural power. An Athenian decree, for example, forbade women to function as midwives. Since it was the prerogative of upper-class obstetricians to sing the hymn of exorcism that banished evil spirits from the presence of the mother and the newborn child, the decree, as far as it was observed, erected a barrier between women and an age-old incentive for the composition of incantations. Men were successful, too, in dominating the formal religious ceremony. Priests often took the place of priestesses and led the thiasos or congregation of women. Men took over the women's religious rites, gradually belittled the power of the mother-goddess, and altered the character of the rites to suit their own needs. They took over the training of the girl choirs and the task of composing music for the choirs to sing. We can see this shift, this transition going on; men taking over women's rites at first dressed like women. For example, at the great Pyanepsia, a food festival or bean feast in which the participants ate a common meal out of a common pot, the men porters dressed as women.

With the taking over of religious festivals—always accompanied by the mimetic rite and music—men removed from women's control the activity that had been since time immemorial the principal incentive for the development of musical imagination. Although women continued to practice rites and to sing religious music in organized choirs, their spiritual activity had but little significance for the group then in control. Even priests had lost some prestige, having defaulted in favor of philosophers and the now rising dramatists.

The most remarkable result of this taking over of the women's rites was the development, out of the choral dances of women's bacchantes at the festival of Dionysos, of the great art form of the Greek tragedy. The Greek tragedy is a choral drama built on the singing and dancing choruses of women. The collective reaction of these choral participants, their philosophical interpretations of each stage of the drama, and their invocations to the deities from time to time make the drama. The actual story of a Greek tragedy is slight. The participants are few and the whole is, from the point of view of modern dramatic technique, rather static. A Greek drama represents what would be only the last act of a modern play. All the preliminary material, all the emotional build-up for the dramatic action, is provided by the choruses. The subject matter is traditional and religious, representing a sophisticated secularization of themes, moral and philosophical concepts and stories, some of which were of immemorial antiquity in the women's rites, many of which had long before been given a finished art form in the women's rituals of Crete.

When men took over the whole basic material of the women's festivals, they made some remarkable changes. In the first place, they transformed them from religious rituals into great popular shows, performed not in the sacred place but on a large stadium. In the second place, they took them entirely out of women's hands, even though to do this, numbers of men performers had to dress as women, to cultivate women's voices and women's ways, and to sacrifice their own virile attributes to a silly feminization of their personalities. Men impersonated the women characters; only men and boys sang in the dramatic choruses. Outside of Athens, in small country communities, women may have participated, but in Athens they possibly did not even attend the performance.

In the third place, the writing of plays and preparations of choruses was thrown open to competition, from which the social seclusion and educational limitations imposed on Athenian women naturally barred them. Hundreds of men playwrights, artists, performers competed in putting on plays. The best were selected by the state and given a great public performance. Here, in the public performance before huge masses of nonparticipating spectators and in the intense competition in technical performance, is the characteristic form of much of modern musical and artistic production. It is in every respect a contrast to the original women's rituals on which Greek tragedy is based, performed often in secret, by women, in the sincere religious outpouring of feeling.

The fourth change the men made when they turned women's choral dances into tragedy is the most remarkable. As has been so often said, it was characteristic of women's sense of pain and sorrow that, while they made the most of it artistically with weeping and wailing, there is also implicit in every woman's ceremony the idea of rebirth. This, from time immemorial, had been the faith of women, the essence of their own observation of other living creatures.

The men who took over the choruses and gave them grandeur,

substance, and a kind of solid dignity had no perception whatever of the woman's faith, because they did not have the unique experience on which it is founded—the monthly cycle, pregnancy, and the supreme agony and triumph of childbirth. They saw the emotional effect of the wail songs and wished to keep it. They devoted a great deal of sound masculine logic to explaining the psychological value of a bath in sorrow. It was, said Aristotle, a form of emotional purification, a purgation of the two great fundamental emotions of terror and pity—terror of one's own fate, pity for that of others. But these men, for all their able and earnest efforts, missed the vital point in the women's sorrow—the hope and the intention of invoking the rebirth. There is no rebirth in Greek tragedy. There is really very little faith. Substantial, solid, and somber, the story moves to its climax in death or destruction.

All that remains in the handling by Greek tragic poets of the material they borrowed from the women's rites is the nobility of the women's characters. Many heroines appear in the dramas. Women characters in the great Greek plays are as numerous, as noble, and as intelligent as the men. They reflect the former power of the principle that female energy is creative and the traditional respect accorded it by the men and women of earlier times. Women's spiritual influence was still recent enough to be a suitable topic for the state players, but women themselves were excluded from this development of their ancient rites.

Sensitive men, who saw what was happening, felt that the stilling of women's voices might be the end of the true life of Greece. And so it actually proved. For after the great age of drama and art, which was the first flowering of men's taking over of women's rites, there was but little more inspiration. Euripides thought the women should not allow this usurpation. He even protested against the physical enforcement of chastity. It is deadly, he said, "to hold maids pure perforce."

"In them it lies, in their own hearts; no bawdy throng can soil the soul of her who knows no wrong!" [13]

He implied in *The Bacchae* that they might rise in their might and take back what was their own. One of the leaders of his rebelling Bacchantes sings:

"With fierce joy I rejoice,
    Child of a savage shore;